Frederic Lawrence Knowles

The Golden Treasury of American Songs and Lyrics

Frederic Lawrence Knowles

The Golden Treasury of American Songs and Lyrics

ISBN/EAN: 9783743312517

Manufactured in Europe, USA, Canada, Australia, Japa

Cover: Foto ©Thomas Meinert / pixelio.de

Manufactured and distributed by brebook publishing software (www.brebook.com)

Frederic Lawrence Knowles

The Golden Treasury of American Songs and Lyrics

The Golden Treasury of Magazine Verse

Edited by
WILLIAM STANLEY BRAITHWAITE

LONDON
GEORGE HARRAP & COMPANY
2-3 PORTSMOUTH STREET, KINGSWAY, W. C.

TO MY FRIEND

Ridgely Torrence

SPIRITUAL POET AND DRAMATIST

FOREWORD

THE selections in this book are gathered from American magazines, during the period from 1905 to 1917, which embrace the editor's studies and summaries of contemporary poetry that have appeared in the BOSTON EVENING TRANSCRIPT. The collection thus in part antedates the present vogue in poetry, while representing the various qualities and schools of the poetic revival in its progress. The magazines, it is clearly wished to be understood, have been the source from which the material is taken. Some of the poems have gone into the authors' books, but a good many remain buried in the files of the various magazines — an ill-deserved fate. It may not seem inappropriate, levying as the editor has upon the late Francis Palgrave's fortunately descriptive title for his anthologies of English songs and lyrics, to call this collection, a "golden treasury" of magazine verse.

If the editor were to make an apology for the omission of any poem that happens to be a favorite with the reader, he would have to make many such to many readers. He can only plead that, tastes and opinions are so various and opposite, were the reader or critic turned editor, he would needs be apologetic, if it were the custom of editors to be so, which it is not. What an editor includes, granting the reader the full exercise of his own opinion, he certainly will not break faith with.

W. S. B.

CAMBRIDGE, MASSACHUSETTS,
March 20, 1918.

ACKNOWLEDGMENTS

To the following publishers thanks are due for permission to include poems that have been issued in books having their copyright:

THE MACMILLAN COMPANY: "The Field of Glory" from "Captain Craig, A Book of Poems," "Flammonde," "The Gift of God," and "Cassandra," from "The Man against the Sky," by Edwin Arlington Robinson; "The Chinese Nightingale," from "The Chinese Nightingale and Other Poems;" "Yankee Doodle" from "The Congo and Other Poems," and "General William Booth Enters into Heaven" from "General William Booth and Other Poems," by Vachel Lindsay; "School" and "Fight" from "The Present Hour, A Book of Poems," by Percy Mackaye; "Barter," "The Broken Field," "The Look," from "Love Songs" by Sara Teasdale; "The Flight" and "Comrades" from "The Flight and Other Poems," by George Edward Woodberry; "Doors," from "Ballads and Poems" by Hermann Hagedorn; "Autochthon" from "The Great Valley" and "Silence" from "Songs and Satires" by Edgar Lee Masters; and "1777" and "Patterns" from "Men, Women and Ghosts," "Hymn to Demeter" and "We Who Were Lovers of Life" from "The Story of Eleusis" by Louis V. Ledoux.

HENRY HOLT AND COMPANY: "The Hill-Wife," "The Death of the Hired Man" from "North of Boston," "The Road not Taken," "Birches" and "The Bonfire" from "Mountain Interval" by Robert Frost; "Emilia" from "Portraits and Protests" by Sara N. Cleghorn.

HARPER AND BROTHERS: "Gayheart, A Story of Defeat," from "Poems" by Dana Burnet.

THE CENTURY COMPANY: "The Night Court," "The Sin Eater" and "St. John of Nepomuc" from "The Night Court and Other Verse," by Ruth Comfort Mitchell; "Landscapes" and "Summors" from "Challenge" by Louis Untermeyer; "We Dead" and "A Handful of Dust," from "Songs for the New Age" by James Oppenheim.

FREDERICK A. STOKES COMPANY: "To a Phoebe-Bird," "Train-Mates" "To No One in Particular," "A Thrush in the Moonlight," from "Grenstone Poems" by Witter Bynner.

CHARLES SCRIBNER'S SONS: "To a Hermit Thrush," "Path-Flower," "Old Fairingdown" from "Path-Flower and Other Poems" by Olive Tilford Dargan; "From a Motor in May" from "One Woman to Another" by Corinne Roosevelt Robinson; and "I Have a Rendezvous with Death" from the "Poems" of Alan Seeger.

HOUGHTON MIFFLIN COMPANY: "The Monk in the Kitchen" and "Grieve not, Ladies" from "Rose of the Wind" by Anna Hempstead Branch; "Cradle-Song," "Harvest Moon: 1914" and "A Dog" from "Harvest Moon" by Josephine Preston Peabody; "A Memorial Tablet" from "The Ride House" by Florence Wilkinson Evans; "Lincoln" from "Some Imagists Poets; 1917" by John Gould Fletcher; "Evensong" from "Turns and Movies" by

ACKNOWLEDGMENTS

Conrad Aiken; "The Adventurer," from "A Lonely Flute" by Odell Shepard; "The King of Dreams" from "Selected Poems" by Clinton Scollard; "With Cassock Black, Baret and Book" from "The Little Gray Songs of St. Josephs" by Grace Fallow Norton; and "The Unconquered Air" and "Indian Pipe" from "Collected Poems" by Florence Earle Coates.

GEORGE H. DORAN COMPANY: "Trees" and "The Twelve-Forty-Five," from "Trees and Other Poems" by Joyce Kilmer; "In the Roman Forum" from "In Deep Places" and "The Poppies" from "Life and Living" by Amelia Josephine Burr.

THE MANAS PRESS: "Cinquains" from "Verses" by Adelaide Crapsey.

D. APPLETON AND COMPANY: "Sleep," from "The Wind in the Corn," by Edith Wyatt.

THE FOUR SEAS COMPANY: "Miracles" from "The Jig of Forslin" by Conrad Aiken; and "Moods" from "A Cabinet of Jade" by David O'Neil.

THE LYRIC PUBLISHING COMPANY: "Ash Wednesday" from "The Shadowed Hour" by John Erskine.

THE LITTLE BOOK PUBLISHER: "The Clerk," from "Streets and Faces," by Scudder Middleton.

THE FRANKLIN PRESS: "He Whom a Dream Hath Possessed," "They Went Forth to Battle, but they Always Fell" from "A Blossomy Bough" and "Thanksgiving for Our Task" from "The Feet of the Goat" by Shaemas O Sheel.

SMALL, MAYNARD AND COMPANY: "Song" and "Magic" from "White Fountains: Odes and Lyrics" by Edward J. O'Brien; and "A Mountain Gateway" from "April Airs" by Bliss Carman.

THE YALE UNIVERSITY PRESS: "The Horse Thief" from "The Burglar of the Zodiac" by William Rose Benét.

G. P. PUTNAMS' SONS: "The Unknown Brothers" and "Letters from Egypt" from "The Shadow of Aetna," by Louis V. Ledoux.

RICHARD G. BADGER: "Grandmither, Think not I Forget," from "April Twilights," by Willa Sibert Cather.

ALFRED A. KNOPF: "The Interpreter" from "Asphalt and Other Poems" by Orrick Johns.

THE MIDLAND PRESS: "Meanwhile" from "Barbed Wire and Other Poems" by Edwin Ford Piper.

SHERMAN, FRENCH AND COMPANY: "Motherhood" from "The Border of the Lake," and "A Statue in a Garden" from "The Sharing," by Agnes Lee.

THE CORNHILL COMPANY: "Over Night, a Rose" from "The Divine Image: A Book of Lyrics" by Caroline Giltinan.

NICHOLAS BROWN: "Samson Allen" from "Nine Poems of a Valetudinarium" by Donald Evans.

THOMAS BIRD MOSHER: "On a copy of Keats' 'Endymion'" from "Lyrics from a Library" by Clinton Scollard; and "Two Songs in Spring" from "The Voice in the Silence" by Thomas S. Jones, Jr.

THE WOODBERRY SOCIETY: "Immortal Love" from "Ideal Passion Sonnets," by George Edward Woodberry.

ACKNOWLEDGMENTS

THE ROADSIDE PRESS: "Coming Home," from "Western Waters," by Elizabeth Sewell Hill.

PUBLISHED BY THE AUTHOR: "November," from "Sonnets: A First Series," by Mahlon Leonard Fisher.

To Ridgely Torrence, Eunice Tietjens, Amy Lowell, Carl Sandburg, Kendall Harrison, John Hall Wheelock, Willa Sibert Cather, Dana Burnet, Karle Wilson Baker, Bliss Carman, Ethel Syford, Anna Spencer Twitchell, James Oppenheim, Frederick Faust, Margaret French Patton, David Morton, Cuthbert Wright, Wallace Stevens, Charles Hanson Towne, Jessie Wallace Hughan, Orrick Johns, Edith Wharton, Dorothea Lawrence Mann, Louise Driscoll, and Katharine Lee Bates, I am indebted for the permission they gave me to include poems not yet collected by them.

To the editors and proprietors of the magazines my thanks are due for permissions to reprint. Under each poem is given the name of the magazine from which it is taken.

CONTENTS

1. BARTER 1
   Sara Teasdale
2. PATH-FLOWER 1
   Olive Tilford Dargan
3. HYMN TO DEMETER 5
   Louis V. Ledoux
4. TO IMAGINATION 6
   Dorothea Lawrence Mann
5. TWO SONGS IN SPRING 8
   Thomas S. Jones, Jr.
6. TREES 9
   Joyce Kilmer
7. LANDSCAPES 9
   Louis Untermeyer
8. TO A HERMIT THRUSH 12
   Olive Tilford Dargan
9. TO A PHŒBE-BIRD 16
   Witter Bynner
10. BIRCHES 16
    Robert Frost
11. INDIAN-PIPE 19
    Florence Earle Coates
12. FROM A MOTOR IN MAY 20
    Corinne Roosevelt Robinson
13. A MOUNTAIN GATEWAY 20
    Bliss Carman
14. THE FLIGHT 22
    George Edward Woodberry

CONTENTS

15. MAGIC 23
    Edward J. O'Brien
16. EARTH 26
    John Hall Wheelock
17. THE ROAD NOT TAKEN 29
    Robert Frost
18. THE ADVENTURER 29
    Odell Shepard
19. GOOD COMPANY 30
    Karle Wilson Baker
20. TO NO ONE IN PARTICULAR 31
    Witter Bynner
21. THE SEA-LANDS 31
    Orrick Johns
22. THE NEW PLATONIST 33
    Cuthbert Wright
23. EMILIA 34
    Sarah N. Cleghorn
24. THE INTERPRETER 36
    Orrick Johns
25. THE LOOK 37
    Sara Teasdale
26. "IMMORTAL LOVE" 37
    George Edward Woodberry
27. PETER QUINCE AT THE CLAVIER 39
    Wallace Stevens
28. THE UNKNOWN BELOVED 42
    John Hall Wheelock
29. PATTERNS 43
    Amy Lowell
30. EVENSONG 46
    Conrad Aiken
31. WAITING 50
    Charles Hanson Towne

CONTENTS

32. THE BROKEN FIELD 51
    Sara Teasdale
33. "GRANDMITHER, THINK NOT I FORGET" 51
    Willa Sibert Cather
34. HUNGARIAN LOVE-LAMENT 53
    Ethel Syford
35. OLD FAIRINGDOWN 54
    Olive Tilford Dargan
36. MOTHERHOOD 58
    Agnes Lee
37. THE HILL WIFE 59
    Robert Frost
38. THE WIFE 62
    Anna Spencer Twitchell
39. NEEDLE TRAVEL 63
    Margaret French Patton
40. CRADLE SONG 65
    Josephine Preston Peabody
41. BACCHANTE TO HER BABE 68
    Eunice Tietjens
42. THE SON 70
    Ridgely Torrence
43. WITH CASSOCK BLACK, BARET AND BOOK 71
    Grace Fallon Norton
44. MOODS 72
    David O'Neil
45. CINQUAINS 74
    Adelaide Crapsey
46. THE REGENTS' EXAMINATION 76
    Jessie Wallace Hughan
47. TRAIN-MATES 76
    Witter Bynner
48. THANKSGIVING FOR OUR TASK 78
    Shaemas O Sheel

CONTENTS

49. SCHOOL 81
    Percy MacKaye
50. YANKEE DOODLE 86
    Vachel Lindsay
51. CASSANDRA 88
    Edwin Arlington Robinson
52. THE BONFIRE 90
    Robert Frost
53. HARVEST-MOON: 1914 94
    Josephine Preston Peabody
54. THE CHINESE NIGHTINGALE 96
    Vachel Lindsay
55. HE WHOM A DREAM HATH POSSESSED . . . 103
    Shaemas O Sheel
56. THE KING OF DREAMS 105
    Clinton Scollard
57. FLAMMONDE 106
    Edwin Arlington Robinson
58. SANDY STAR 109
    William Stanley Braithwaite
59. SAINT JOHN OF NEPOMUC 112
    Ruth Comfort Mitchell
60. SAMSON ALLEN 116
    Donald Evans
61. GAYHEART 117
    Dana Burnet
62. THE UNCONQUERED AIR 131
    Florence Earle Coates
63. A LIKENESS 132
    Willa Sibert Cather
64. ON A COPY OF KEATS' "ENDYMION" . . . 134
    Clinton Scollard
65. SILENCE 136
    Edgar Lee Masters

CONTENTS

66. MIRACLES 139
    Conrad Aiken
67. ASH WEDNESDAY 143
    John Erskine
68. TO A LOGICIAN 150
    Dana Burnet
69. THE CLERK 151
    Scudder Middleton
70. A DOG 152
    Josephine Preston Peabody
71. THE NIGHT COURT 154
    Ruth Comfort Mitchell
72. GUNS AS KEYS: AND THE GREAT GATE SWINGS . . 157
    Amy Lowell
73. THE FIELD OF GLORY 184
    Edwin Arlington Robinson
74. FIGHT 186
    Percy MacKaye
75. THE HORSE THIEF 201
    William Rose Benét
76. THE BIRD AND THE TREE 207
    Ridgely Torrence
77. 1777 208
    Amy Lowell
78. LETTERS FROM EGYPT 215
    Louis V. Ledoux
79. IN THE ROMAN FORUM 215
    Amelia Josephine Burr
80. THE SIN EATER 217
    Ruth Comfort Mitchell
81. EYE-WITNESS 220
    Ridgely Torrence
82. THE GIFT OF GOD 227
    Edwin Arlington Robinson

CONTENTS

83. MEANWHILE 228
    Edwin Ford Piper
84. GRIEVE NOT, LADIES 232
    Anna Hempstead Branch
85. COOL TOMBS 233
    Carl Sandburg
86. MEMORIES OF WHITMAN AND LINCOLN 234
    James Oppenheim
87. AUTOCHTHON 238
    Edgar Lee Masters
88. LINCOLN 247
    John Gould Fletcher
89. GENERAL WILLIAM BOOTH ENTERS INTO HEAVEN . 250
    Vachel Lindsay
90. THE POPPIES 253
    Amelia Josephine Burr
91. YELLOW CLOVER 255
    Katharine Lee Bates
92. OVER NIGHT, A ROSE 258
    Caroline Giltinan
93. EVENSONG 259
    Ridgely Torrence
94. BATTLE SLEEP 260
    Edith Wharton
95. SONG 261
    Edward J. O'Brien
96. A STATUE IN A GARDEN 261
    Agnes Lee
97. THE LESSER CHILDREN 262
    Ridgely Torrence
98. A THRUSH IN THE MOONLIGHT 269
    Witter Bynner
99. NOVEMBER 269
    Mahlon Leonard Fisher

CONTENTS

- 100. THE WINTER SCENE 270
   Bliss Carman
- 101. THE TWELVE-FORTY-FIVE 272
   Joyce Kilmer
- 102. COMING HOME 275
   Elizabeth Sewell Hill
- 103. WE WHO WERE LOVERS OF LIFE 278
   Louis V. Ledoux
- 104. SUMMONS 280
   Louis Untermeyer
- 105. THE DEAD 282
   David Morton
- 106. WE DEAD 283
   James Oppenheim
- 107. TO A DEAD SOLDIER 288
   Kendall Harrison
- 108. THE DEATH OF THE HIRED MAN 288
   Robert Frost
- 109. A HANDFUL OF DUST 295
   James Oppenheim
- 110. "I HAVE A RENDEZVOUS WITH DEATH" 296
   Alan Seeger
- 111. THE SECRET 297
   Frederick Faust
- 112. SCINTILLA 299
   William Stanley Braithwaite
- 113. SLEEP 299
   Edith Wyatt
- 114. A MEMORIAL TABLET 302
   Florence Wilkinson Evans
- 115. EPITAPH 303
   Louise Driscoll
- 116. COMRADES 305
   George Edward Woodberry

CONTENTS

117. THEY WENT FORTH TO BATTLE BUT THEY ALWAYS FELL 307
    Shaemas O Sheel
118. THE UNKNOWN BROTHERS 308
    Louis V. Ledoux
119. THE MONK IN THE KITCHEN 310
    Anna Hempstead Branch
120. DOORS 314
    Hermann Hagedorn

INDEX OF AUTHORS 315
INDEX OF POEMS 317
INDEX OF FIRST LINES 321

The
Golden Treasury of
Magazine Verse

Barter

LIFE has loveliness to sell —
   All beautiful and splendid things,
Blue waves whitened on a cliff,
   Climbing fire that sways and sings,
And children's faces looking up
Holding wonder like a cup.

Life has loveliness to sell —
   Music like a curve of gold,
Scent of pine trees in the rain,
   Eyes that love you, arms that hold,
And for your spirit's still delight,
Holy thoughts that star the night.

Spend all you have for loveliness,
   Buy it and never count the cost;
For one white singing hour of peace
   Count many a year of strife well lost,
And for a breath of ecstasy
Give all you have been or could be.

Poetry: A Magazine of Verse   Sara Teasdale

Path-Flower

A RED-CAP sang in Bishop's wood,
   A lark o'er Golder's lane,
As I the April pathway trod
   Bound west for Willesden.

At foot each tiny blade grew big
   And taller stood to hear.
And every leaf on every twig
   Was like a little ear.

As I too paused, and both ways tried
   To catch the rippling rain, —
So still, a hare kept at my side
   His tussock of disdain, —

Behind me close I heard a step,
   A soft pit-pat surprise,
And looking round my eyes fell deep
   Into sweet other eyes;

The eyes like wells, where sun lies too,
   So clear and trustful brown,
Without a bubble warning you
   That here's a place to drown.

"How many miles?" Her broken shoes
   Had told of more than one.
She answered like a dreaming Muse,
   "I came from Islington."

"So long a tramp?" Two gentle nods,
   Then seemed to lift a wing,
And words fell soft as willow-buds,
   "I came to find the Spring."

A timid voice, yet not afraid
   In ways so sweet to roam,
As it with honey bees had played
   And could no more go home.

Her home! I saw the human lair,
  I heard the hucksters bawl,
I stifled with the thickened air
  Of bickering mart and stall.

Without a tuppence for a ride,
  Her feet had set her free.
Her rags, that decency defied,
  Seemed new with liberty.

But she was frail. Who would might note
  That trail of hungering
That for an hour she had forgot
  In wonder of the Spring.

So shriven by her joy she glowed
  It seemed a sin to chat.
"A tea-shop snuggled off the road;"
  Why did I think of that?

Oh, frail, so frail! I could have wept, —
  But she was passing on,
And I but muddled, "You'll accept
  A penny for a bun?"

Then up her little throat a spray
  Of rose climbed, for it must;
A wilding lost till safe it lay
  Hid by her curls of rust;

And I saw modesties at fence
  With pride that bore no name;
So old it was she knew not whence
  It sudden woke and came;

But that which shone of all most clear
    Was startled, sadder thought
That I should give her back the fear
    Of life she had forgot.

And I blushed for the world we'd made,
    Putting God's hand aside,
Till for the want of sun and shade
    His little children died;

And blushed that I who every year
    With Spring went up and down,
Must greet a soul that ached for her
    With "penny for a bun!"

Struck as a thief in holy place
    Whose sin upon him cries,
I watched the flowers leave her face,
    The song go from her eyes.

Then she, sweet heart, she saw my rout,
    And of her charity
A hand of grace put softly out
    And took the coin from me.

A red-cap sang in Bishop's wood,
    A lark o'er Golder's lane;
But I, alone, still glooming stood,
    And April plucked in vain;

Till living words rang in my ears
    And sudden music played:
Out of such sacred thirst as hers
    The world shall be remade.

Afar she turned her head and smiled
   As might have smiled the Spring,
And humble as a wondering child
   I watched her vanishing.
The Atlantic Monthly   Olive Tilford Dargan

3   *Hymn to Demeter*

From "The Story of Eleusis"

WEAVE the dance, and raise again the sacred chorus;
   Wreathe the garlands of the spring about the hair;
Now once more the meadows burst in bloom before us,
   Crying swallows dart and glitter through the air.
Glints the plowshare in the brown and fragrant furrow;
   Pigeons coo in shady coverts as they pair;
Come the furtive mountain folk from cave and burrow,
   Lean, and blinking at the sunlight's sudden glare.

Bright through midmost heaven moves the lesser Lion;
   Hide the Hyades in ocean caverns hoar;
Past the shoulders of the sunset flames Orion,
   Following the sisters seaward evermore.
Gleams the east at evening, lit by low Arcturus;
   Out to subtle-scented dawns beside the shore,
Yet a little and the Pleiades will lure us:
   Weave the dance and raise the chorus as of yore.

Far to eastward up the fabled gulf of Issus,
   Northward, southward, westward, now the trader goes,
Passing headlands clustered yellow with narcissus,
   Bright with hyacinth, with poppy, and with rose.

Shines the sea and falls the billow as undaunted,
   Past the rising of the stars that no man knows,
Sails he onward through the islands siren-haunted,
   Till the clashing gates of rock before him close.

Kindly Mother of the beasts and birds and flowers,
   Gracious bringer of the barley and the grain,
Earth awakened feels thy sunlight and thy showers;
   Great Demeter! Let us call thee not in vain;
Lead us safely from the seedtime to the threshing,
   Past the harvest and the vineyard's purple stain;
Let us see thy corn-pale hair the sunlight meshing,
   When the sounding flails of autumn swing again.
The Yale Review   Louis V. Ledoux

4   *To Imagination*

[Suggested by Maxfield Parrish's "Air Castles"]

O BEAUTEOUS boy a-dream, what visions sought
   Of pictures magical thy eyes unfold,
What triumphs of celestial wonders wrought,
   What marvels from a breath of beauty rolled!
Skyward and seaward on the clouds are scrolled
   A mystic imagery of castled thought,
A thousand worlds to lose, — or win and mold, —
   A radiant iridescence swiftly caught
Of ever-changing glory, fancy-fraught.

Blue wonder of the sea and luminous sky, —
   A thousand wonders in thy dreamlit face, —
Eyes that beheld afar the turrets high
   Of Ilium, and the transient mortal grace

OF MAGAZINE VERSE

Of Deirdre's sadness, all the conquering race
  Of Athens, — eyes that saw Eden's beauty lie
In passionate adoration — visions trace
  Across the tender brooding of the sigh
That wrecked a city and made chieftains die.

Forward not backward turns the mystic shine
  Of those far-seeing orbs that track the gleam —
The fleecy marvel of the cloud is line
  On line the wizard tracery of a dream.
O lad, who buildest not of things that seem,
  Beyond what bounds of visioning divine
Came that far smile, from what long-strayed sunbeam
  Caught thou the radiance, from what fostering vine
The power to build and mold the deep design?

Knowest thou the secret that thy brush would tell,
  Is all the dream a bubbled splendor white,
Beyond those castles cloud-bound, does there dwell
  The eternal silence of the dark — or light?
Will thy hand hold the pen which shall indict
  The symbolled mystery — write the final knell
Of rainbow fancy — is the distant sight
  A nothingness encircled by the spell
Of gleaming bubbles wrought of beauty's shell?

In vain to question, where the mystery
  Of Youth's short golden dream is lord and king.
The eyes that farthest gaze in ecstasy,
  Were never meant to paint the immortal thing
They see, nor understand the joy they bring.
  The misty baubles of the sky and sea

Sail on. Dream still, bright-visioned boy, and fling
   The glittering mantle of thy thoughts that flee,
Weaving us evermore thy shining pageantry.
The Poetry Journal   *Dorothea Lawrence Mann*

Two Songs in Spring

I

O LITTLE buds all bourgeoning with Spring,
   You hold my winter in forgetfulness;
Without my window lilac branches swing,
Within my gate I hear a robin sing —
   O little laughing blooms that lift and bless!

So blow the breezes in a soft caress,
   Blowing my dreams upon a swallow's wing;
O little merry buds in dappled dress,
You fill my heart with very wantonness —
   O little buds all bourgeoning with Spring!

II

At hint of Spring I have you back again —
   The blush of apple-blossoms on the bough,
A scent of buds far sweeter for the rain . . .
At hint of Spring I have you back again,
   And all the time is lost since then and now.

Your voice is hidden in the thrush's song,
   And in the south wind's slumbering refrain;

You needs must come, love is so very strong,
And we who found each other waited long —
   At hint of Spring I have you back again!
The Pathfinder   *Thomas S. Jones, Jr.*

Trees

I THINK that I shall never see
   A poem lovely as a tree.

A tree whose hungry mouth is prest
Against the sweet earth's sweet flowing breast;

A tree that looks at God all day
And lifts her leafy arms to pray;

A tree that may in Summer wear
A nest of robins in her hair;

Upon whose bosom snow has lain;
Who intimately lives with rain.

Poems are made by fools like me,
But only God can make a tree!
Poetry: A Magazine of Verse   *Joyce Kilmer*

Landscapes

(*For Clement R. Wood*)

THE rain was over, and the brilliant air
   Made every little blade of grass appear
Vivid and startling — everything was there
With sharpened outlines, eloquently clear,
As though one saw it in a crystal sphere.

The rusty sumac with its struggling spires;
The golden-rod with all its million fires;
(A million torches swinging in the wind)
A single poplar, marvellously thinned,
Half like a naked boy, half like a sword;
Clouds, like the haughty banners of the Lord;
A group of pansies with their shrewish faces
Little old ladies cackling over laces;
The quaint, unhurried road that curved so well;
The prim petunias with their rich, rank smell;
The lettuce-birds, the creepers in the field —
How bountifully were they all revealed!
How arrogantly each one seemed to thrive —
So frank and strong, so radiantly alive!

And over all the morning-minded earth
There seemed to spread a sharp and kindling mirth,
Piercing the stubborn stones until I saw
The toad face heaven without shame or awe,
The ant confront the stars, and every weed
Grow proud as though it bore a royal seed;
While all the things that die and decompose
Sent forth their bloom as richly as the rose . . .
Oh, what a liberal power that made them thrive
And keep the very dirt that died, alive.

And now I saw the slender willow-tree
No longer calm or drooping listlessly,
Letting its languid branches sway and fall
As though it danced in some sad ritual;
But rather like a young, athletic girl,
Fearless and gay, her hair all out of curl,

And flying in the wind — her head thrown back,
Her arms flung up, her garments flowing slack,
And all her rushing spirits running over . . .
What made a sober tree seem such a rover —
Or made the staid and stalwart apple-trees,
That stood for years knee-deep in velvet peace,
Turn all their fruit to little worlds of flame,
And burn the trembling orchard there below.
What lit the heart of every golden-glow —
Oh, why was nothing weary, dull or tame? . . .
Beauty it was, and keen, compassionate mirth
That drives the vast and energetic earth.

And, with abrupt and visionary eyes,.
I saw the huddled tenements arise.
Here where the merry clover danced and shone
Sprang agonies of iron and of stone;
There, where the green Silence laughed or stood enthralled,
Cheap music blared and evil alleys sprawled.
The roaring avenues, the shrieking mills;
Brothels and prisons on those kindly hills —
The menace of these things swept over me;
A threatening, unconquerable sea. . . .

A stirring landscape and a generous earth!
Freshening courage and benevolent mirth —
And then the city, like a hideous sore . . .
Good God, and what is all this beauty for?
    The Century Magazine   *Louis Untermeyer*

8   *To a Hermit Thrush*

DWELLER among leaves, and shining twilight boughs
   That fold cool arms about thine altar place,
What joyous race
Of gods dost serve with such unfaltering vows?

Weave me a time-fringed tale
Of slumbering, haunted trees,
And star-sweet fragrances
No day defiled;
Of bowering nights innumerable,
And nestling hours breath-nigh a dryad's heart
That sleeping yet was wild
With dream-beat that thou mad'st a part
Of thy dawn-fluting; ay, and keep'st it still,
Striving so late these godless woods to fill
With undefeated strain,
And in one hour build the old world again.

Wast thou found singing when Diana drew
Her skirts from the first night?
Didst feel the sun-breath when the valleys grew
Warm with the love of light,
Till blades of flower-lit green gave to the wind
The mystery that made sweet
The earth forever, — strange and undefined
As life, as God, as this thy song complete
That holds with me twin memories
Of time ere men,
And ere our ways
Lay sundered with the abyss of air between?

OF MAGAZINE VERSE

List, I will lay
The world, my song,
Deep in the heart of day,
Day that is long
As the ages dream or the stars delay!
Keep thou from me,
Sigh-throated man,
Forever to be
Under the songless wanderer's ban.
I am of time
That counteth no dawn;
Thy æons yet climb
To skies I have won,
Seeking for aye an unrisen sun!

Soft as a shadow slips
Before the moon, I creep beneath the trees,
Even to the boughs whose lowest circling tips
Whisper with the anemones
Thick-strewn as though a cloud had made
Its drifting way through spray and leafy braid
And sunk with unremembering ease
To humbler heaven upon the mossy heaps.
And here a warmer flow
Urges thy melody, yet keeps
The cool of bowers; as might a rose blush through
Its unrelinquished dew;
Or bounteous heart that knows not woe,
Put on the robe of sighs, and fain
Would hold in love's surmise a neighbour's pain.

Ah, I have wronged thee, sprite!
So tender now thy song in flight,

So sweet its lingerings are,
It seems the liquid memory
Of time when thou didst try
Thy gleaning wing through human years,
And met, ay, knew the sigh
Of men who pray, the tears
That hide the woman's star,
The brave ascending fire
That is youth's beacon and too soon his pyre, —
Yea, all our striving, bateless and unseeing,
That builds each day our Heaven new.
More deep in time's unnearing blue,
Farther and ever fleeing
The dream that ever must pursue.

*Heart-need is sorest
When the song dies:
Come to the forest,
Brother of the sighs.
Heart-need is song-need,
Brother, give me thine!
Song-meed is heart-meed,
Brother, take mine!*

*I go the still way,
Cover me with night;
Thou goest the will way
Into the light.
Dust and the burden
Thou shalt outrun;
Bear then my guerdon,
Song, to the sun!*

OF MAGAZINE VERSE

O little pagan with the heart of Christ,
I go bewildered from thine altar place,
These brooding boughs and grey-lit forest wings,
Nor know if thou deniest
My destiny and race,
Man's goalward falterings,
To sing the perfect joy that lay
Along the path we missed somewhere,
That led thee to thy home in air,
While we, soil-creepers, bruise our way
Toward heights and sunrise bounds
That wings may know nor feet may win
For all their scars, for all their wounds;
Or have I heard within thy strain
Not sorrow's self, but sorrowing
That thou didst seek the way more free,
Nor took with us the trail of pain
That endeth not, e'er widening
To life that knows what Life may be;
And e'er thou fall'st to silence long
Would golden parting fling:

Go, man, through death unto thy star;
I journey not so far;
My wings must fail e'en with my song.

 Scribner's Magazine   Olive Tilford Dargan

9   *To a Phœbe-Bird*

UNDER the eaves, out of the wet,
   You nest within my reach;
You never sing for me and yet
   You have a golden speech.

You sit and quirk a rapid tail,
   Wrinkle a ragged crest,
Then pirouette from tree to rail
   And vault from rail to nest.

And when in frequent, dainty fright
   You grayly slip and fade,
And when at hand you re-alight
   Demure and unafraid,

And when you bring your brood its fill
   Of iridescent wings
And green legs dewy in your bill,
   Your silence is what sings.

Not of a feather that enjoys
   To prate or praise or preach,
O Phœbe, with so little noise,
   What eloquence you teach!

The Bellman   *Witter Bynner*

10   *Birches*

WHEN I see birches bend to left and right
   Across the lines of straighter darker trees,
I like to think some boy's been swinging them.
But swinging does n't bend them down to stay.

Ice-storms do that. Often you must have seen them
Loaded with ice a sunny winter morning
After a rain. They click upon themselves
As the breeze rises, and turn many-colored
As the stir cracks and crazes their enamel.
Soon the sun's warmth makes them shed crystal shells
Shattering and avalanching on the snow-crust —
Such heaps of broken glass to sweep away
You'd think the inner dome of heaven had fallen.
They are dragged to the withered bracken by the load
And they seem not to break; though once they are bowed

So low for long they never right themselves:
You may see their trunks arching in the woods
Years afterwards, trailing their leaves on the ground
Like girls on hands and knees that throw their hair
Before them over their heads to dry in the sun.
But I was going to say when truth broke in
With all her matter-of-fact about the ice-storm,
(Now am I free to be poetical?)
I should prefer to have some boy bend them
As he went out and in to fetch the cows —
Some boy too far from town to learn baseball,
Whose only play was what he found himself,
Summer or winter, and could play alone.
One by one he subdued his father's trees
By riding them down over and over again
Until he took the stiffness out of them
And not one but hung limp, not one was left
For him to conquer. He learned all there was
To learn about not launching out too soon
And so not carrying the tree away

THE GOLDEN TREASURY

Clear to the ground. He always kept his poise
To the top branches, climbing carefully
With the same pains you use to fill a cup
Up to the brim, and even above the brim.
Then he flung outward, feet first, with a swish,
Kicking his way down through the air to the ground.
So was I once myself a swinger of birches.
And so I dream of going back to be.
It's when I'm weary of considerations,
And life is too much like a pathless wood
Where your face burns and tickles with the cobwebs
Broken across it, and one eye is weeping
From a twig's having lashed across it open.
I'd like to get away from earth awhile
And then come back to it and begin over.
May no fate willfully misunderstand me
And half grant what I wish and snatch me away
Not to return. Earth's the right place for love:
I don't know where it's likely to go better.
I'd like to go by climbing a birch tree,
And climb black branches up a snow-white trunk
Toward heaven, till the tree could bear no more,
But dipped its top and set me down again.
That would be good both going and coming back.
One could do worse than be a swinger of birches.
   The Atlantic Monthly   *Robert Frost*

11   *Indian-Pipe*

IN the heart of the forest arising,
   Slim, ghostly, and fair,
Ethereal offspring of moisture,
   Of earth and of air;
With slender stems anchored together
   Where first they uncurl,
Each tipped with its exquisite lily
   Of mother-of-pearl;
Mid the pine-needles, closely enwoven
   Its roots to embale, —
The Indian-pipe of the woodland,
   Thrice lovely and frail!

Is this but an earth-springing fungus —
   This darling of Fate
Which out of the moulding darkness
   Such light can create?
Or is it the spirit of Beauty,
   Here drawn by love's lure
To give to the forest a something
   Unearthy and pure:
To crystallize dewdrop and balsam
   And dryad-lisped words
And starbeam and moonrise and rapture
   And song of wild birds?

Harper's Magazine   *Florence Earle Coates*

12   *From a Motor in May*

THE leaves of Autumn and the buds of Spring
    Meet and commingle on our winding way —
And we, who glide into the heart of May,
Sense in our souls a sudden quivering.
What though the flash of blue or scarlet wing
Bid us forget the night in dawning day,
Skies of November, sullen, sad, and gray,
Once hung above this withered covering.
There is no Spring that Autumn has not known,
Nor any Autumn Spring has not divined, —
The odor of dead flowers on the wind
Shall but enrich a fairer blossoming,
And though they shiver from a breeze outblown,
The leaves of Autumn guard the buds of Spring.
The Outlook   *Corinne Roosevelt Robinson*

13   *A Mountain Gateway*

I KNOW a vale where I would go one day,
    When June comes back and all the world once more
Is glad with summer. Deep with shade it lies,
A mighty cleft in the green bosoming hills,
A cool, dim gateway to the mountains' heart.

On either side the wooded slopes come down,
Hemlock and beech and chestnut; here and there
Through the deep forest laurel spreads and gleams,
Pink-white as Daphne in her loveliness —

That still perfection from the world withdrawn,
As if the wood gods had arrested there
Immortal beauty in her breathless flight.

Far overhead against the arching blue
Gray ledges overhang from dizzy heights,
Scarred by a thousand winters and untamed.
The road winds in from the broad riverlands,
Luring the happy traveler turn by turn,
Up to the lofty mountains of the sky.

And where the road runs in the valley's foot,
Through the dark woods the mountain stream comes
    down,
Singing and dancing all its youth away
Among the boulders and the shallow runs,
Where sunbeams pierce and mossy tree trunks hang,
Drenched all day long with murmuring sound and spray.
There, light of heart and footfree, I would go
Up to my home among the lasting hills,
And in my cabin doorway sit me down,
Companioned in that leafy solitude
By the wood ghosts of twilight and of peace.

And in that sweet seclusion I should hear,
Among the cool-leafed beeches in the dusk,
The calm-voiced thrushes at their evening hymn —
So undistraught, so rapturous, so pure,
It well might be, in wisdom and in joy,
The seraphs singing at the birth of time
The unworn ritual of eternal things.

The Smart Set   *Bliss Carman*

14 *The Flight*

O WILD Heart, track the land's perfume,
    Beach-roses and moor-heather!
All fragrances of herb and bloom
    Fail, out at sea, together.
O follow where aloft find room
    Lark-song and eagle-feather!
All ecstasies of throat and plume
    Melt, high on yon blue weather.

O leave on sky and ocean lost
    The flight creation dareth;
Take wings of love, that mounts the most;
    Find fame, that furthest fareth!
Thy flight, albeit amid her host
    Thee, too, night star-like beareth,
Flying, thy breast on heaven's coast,
    The infinite outweareth.

II

"Dead o'er us roll celestial fires;
    Mute stand Earth's ancient beaches;
Old thoughts, old instincts, old desires,
    The passing hour outreaches;
The soul creative never tires —
    Evokes, adores, beseeches;
And that heart most the god inspires
    Whom most its wildness teaches.

"For I will course through falling years,
    And stars and cities burning;

And I will march through dying cheers
    Past empires unreturning;
Ever the world-flame reappears
    Where mankind power is earning,
The nations' hopes, the people's tears,
    One with the wild heart yearning."
Scribner's Magazine   George Edward Woodberry

15   *Magic*

I RAN into the sunset light
  As hard as I could run:
The treetops bowed in sheer delight
As if they loved the sun:
And all the songs of little birds
Who laughed and cried in silver words
Were joined as they were one.

And down the streaming golden sky
A lark came circling with a cry
Of wonder-weaving joy:
And all the arch of heaven rang
Where meadowlands of dreaming hang
As when I was a boy.

And through the ringing solitude
In pulsing lovely amplitude
A mist hung in a shroud,
As though the light of loneliness
Turned pure delight to holiness,
And bathed it in a cloud.

I stripped my laughing body bare
And plunged into that holy air
That washed me like a sea,
And raced against its silver tide
That stroked my eager glancing side
And made my spirit free.

Across the limits of the land
The wind and I swept hand in hand
Beyond the golden glow.
We danced across the ocean plain
Like thrushes singing in the rain
A song of long ago.

And on into the silver night
We strove to win the race with light
And bring the vision home,
And bring the wonder home again
Unto the sleeping eyes of men
Across the singing foam.

And down the river of the world
Our glowing limbs in glory swirled
As spring within a flower,
And stars in music of delight
Streamed gaily down our shoulders white
Like petals in a shower.

And tears of awful wonder ran
Adown my cheeks to hear the clan
Of beauty chaunting white

OF MAGAZINE VERSE

The prayer too deep for living word,
Or sight of man, or winging bird,
Or music over forest heard
At falling of the night.

And dropping slowly as the dew
On grasses that the winds renew
In urge of flooding fire,
And softly as the hushing boughs
The gentle airs of dawn arouse
To cradle morning's quire,

The murmur of the singing leaves
Around the secret Flame,
Like mating swallows 'neath the eaves
In rustling silence came,
And flowing through the silent air
Creation fluttered in a prayer
Descending on a spiral stair,
And calling me by name.

It nestled in my dreaming eyes
Like heaven in a lake,
And softened hope into surprise
For very beauty's sake,
And silence blossomed into morn,
Whose fragrant rosy-breasted dawn
Could scarcely bear to break.

I sang into the morning light
As loud as I could sing,
The treetops bowed in sheer delight
Before a slanting wing,

25

And all the songs of little birds
Who laughed and cried in silver words
Adored the Risen Spring.
The Trimmed Lamp   *Edward J. O'Brien*

16   *Earth*

GRASSHOPPER, your fairy song
And my poem alike belong
To the deep and silent earth
From which all poetry has birth;
All we say and all we sing
Is but as the murmuring
Of that drowsy heart of hers
When from her deep dream she stirs:
If we sorrow, or rejoice,
You and I are but her voice.

Deftly does the dust express
In mind her hidden loveliness,
And from her cool silence stream
The cricket's cry and Dante's dream:
For the earth that breeds the trees
Breeds cities too, and symphonies,
Equally her beauty flows
Into a savior, or a rose —
Looks down in dream, and from above
Smiles at herself in Jesus' love.
Christ's love and Homer's art
Are but the workings of her heart;

Through Leonardo's hand she seeks
Herself, and through Beethoven speaks
In holy thunderings around
The awful message of the ground.

The serene and humble mould
Does in herself all selves enfold —
Kingdoms, destinies, and creeds,
Great dreams and dauntless deeds,
Science that metes the firmament,
The high, inflexible intent
Of one for many sacrificed —
Plato's brain, the heart of Christ:
All love, all legend, and all lore
Are in the dust forevermore.

Even as the growing grass
Up from the soil religions pass,
And the field that bears the rye
Bears parables and prophecy.
Out of the earth the poem grows
Like the lily, or the rose;
And all man is, or yet may be,
Is but herself in agony
Toiling up the steep ascent
Towards the complete accomplishment
When all dust shall be, the whole
Universe, one conscious soul.

Yea, the quiet and cool sod
Bears in her breast the dream of God.

If you would know what earth is, scan
The intricate, proud heart of man,
Which is the earth articulate,
And learn how holy and how great,
How limitless and how profound
Is the nature of the ground —
How without terror or demur
We may entrust ourselves to her
When we are wearied out, and lay
Our faces in the common clay.

For she is pity, she is love,
All wisdom she, all thoughts that move
About her everlasting breast
Till she gathers them to rest:
All tenderness of all the ages,
Seraphic secrets of the sages,
Vision and hope of all the seers,
All prayer, all anguish, and all tears
Are but the dust, that from her dream
Awakes, and knows herself supreme —
Are but earth when she reveals
All that her secret heart conceals
Down in the dark and silent loam,
Which is ourselves asleep, at home.

Yea, and this my poem, too,
Is part of her as dust and dew,
Wherein herself she doth declare
Through my lips, and say her prayer.

The Yale Review   *John Hall Wheelock*

17   *The Road not Taken*

TWO roads diverged in a yellow wood,
  And sorry I could not travel both
And be one traveler, long I stood
And looked down one as far as I could
To where it bent in the undergrowth;

Then took the other, as just as fair,
And having perhaps the better claim
Because it was grassy and wanted wear,
Though as for that the passing there
Had worn them really about the same,

And both that morning equally lay
In leaves no step had trodden black.
Oh, I marked the first for another day!
Yet knowing how way leads on to way
I doubted if I should ever come back.

I shall be telling this with a sigh
Somewhere ages and ages hence:
Two roads diverged in a wood, and I,
I took the one less traveled by,
And that has made all the difference.
The Atlantic Monthly   Robert Frost

18   *The Adventurer*

HE did not come in the red dawn,
  Nor in the blaze of noon,
And all the long bright highway
  Lay lonely to the moon,

And nevermore, we know now,
  Will he come wandering down
The breezy hollows of the hills
  That gird the quiet town.

For he has heard a voice cry
  A starry-faint "Ahoy!"
Far up the wind, and followed
  Unquestioning after joy.

But we are long forgetting
  The quiet way he went,
With looks of love and gentle scorn
  So sweetly, subtly blent.

We cannot cease to wonder,
  We who have loved him, how
He fares along the windy ways
  His feet must travel now.

But we must draw the curtain
  And fasten bolt and bars
And talk here in the firelight
  Of him beneath the stars.

The Bellman   *Odell Shepard*

19   Good Company

TO-DAY I have grown taller from walking with the trees,
The seven sister-poplars who go softly in a line;
And I think my heart is whiter for its parley with a star
That trembled out at nightfall and hung above the pine.

The call-note of a redbird from the cedars in the dusk
Woke his happy mate within me to an answer free and fine;
And a sudden angel beckoned from a column of blue
    smoke —
Lord, who am I that they should stoop — these holy folk of
    thine?
    The Poetry Review of America   *Karle Wilson Baker*

20   *To No One in Particular*

LOCATE your love, you lose your love,
    Find her, you look away. . .
Now mine I never quite discern,
    I trace her every day.

She has a thousand presences,
    As surely seen and heard
As birds that hide behind a leaf
    Or leaves that hide a bird.

Single your love, you lose your love,
    You cloak her face with clay;
Now mine I never quite discern —
    And never look away.
    Poetry: A Magazine of Verse   *Witter Bynner*

21   *The Sea-Lands*

WOULD I were on the sea-lands,
    Where winds know how to sting;
And in the rocks at midnight
    The lost long murmurs sing.

Would I were with my first love
    To hear the rush and roar
Of spume below the doorstep
    And winds upon the door.

My first love was a fair girl
    With ways forever new;
And hair a sunlight yellow,
    And eyes a morning blue.

The roses, have they tarried
    Or are they dun and frayed?
If we had stayed together,
    Would love, indeed, have stayed?

Ah, years are filled with learning,
    And days are leaves of change!
And I have met so many
    I knew . . . and found them strange.

But on the sea-lands tumbled
    By winds that sting and blind,
The nights we watched, so silent,
    Come back, come back to mind.

I mind about my first love,
    And hear the rush and roar
Of spume below the doorstep
    And winds upon the door.

The Forum   *Orrick Johns*

The New Platonist
Circa 1640

OUR loves as flowers fall to dust;
   The noblest singing hath an end;
No man to his own soul may trust,
   Nor to the kind arms of his friend;
Yet have I glimpsed by lonely tree,
Bright baths of immortality.

My faultless teachers bid me fare
   The cypress path of blood and tears,
Treading the thorny wold to where
   The painful Cross of Christ appears;
'Twas on another, sunnier hill,
I met you first, my miracle.

The painted windows burn and flame
   Up through the music-haunted air;
These were my gods — and then you came,
   With flowers crowned and sun-kissed hair,
Making this northern river seem
Some laughter-girdled Grecian stream.

When the fierce foeman of our race
   Marshals his lords of lust and pride,
You spring within a moment's space,
   Full-armed and smiling to my side.
O golden heart! The love you gave me,
Alone has saved, and yet will save me.

Perchance we have no perfect city
    Beyond the wrack of these our wars,
Till Death alone in sacred pity
    Wash with long sleep our wounds and scars;
So much the more I praise in measure
The generous gods for you, my treasure.
The New Republic   *Cuthbert Wright*

23   *Emilia*

HALFWAY up the Hemlock valley turnpike,
    In the bend of Silver Water's arm,
Where the deer come trooping down at even,
    Drink the cowslip pool, and fear no harm,
        Dwells Emilia,
Flower of the fields of Camlot Farm.

Sitting sewing by the western window
    As the too brief mountain sunshine flies,
Hast thou seen a slender-shouldered figure
    With a chestnut braid, Minerva-wise,
        Round her temples,
Shadowing her gray, enchanted eyes?

When the freshets flood the Silver Water,
    When the swallow flying northward braves
Sleeting rains that sweep the birchen foothills
    Where the wildflowers' pale plantation waves —
        (Fairy gardens
Springing from the dead leaves in their graves), —

Falls forgotten, then, Emilia's needle;
  Ancient ballads, fleeting through her brain,
Sing the cuckoo and the English primrose,
  Outdoors calling with a quaint refrain;
    And a rainbow
  Seems to brighten through the gusty rain.

Forth she goes, in some old dress and faded,
  Fearless of the showery, shifting wind;
Kilted are her skirts to clear the mosses,
  And her bright braids in a 'kerchief pinned,
    Younger sister
  Of the damsel-errant Rosalind.

When she helps to serve the harvest supper
  In the lantern-lighted village hall,
Moonlight rises on the burning woodland,
  Echoes dwindle from the distant Fall.
    Hark, Emilia!
  In her ear the airy voices call.

Hidden papers in the dusky garret,
  Where her few and secret poems lie, —
Thither flies her heart to join her treasure,
  While she serves, with absent-musing eye,
    Mighty tankards
  Foaming cider in the glasses high.

"Would she mingle with her young companions!"
  Vainly do her aunts and uncles say;
Ever, from the village sports and dances,
  Early missed, Emilia slips away.
    Whither vanished?
  With what unimagined mates to play?

Did they seek her, wandering by the water,
    They should find her comrades shy and strange:
Queens and princesses, and saints and fairies,
    Dimly moving in a cloud of change:
        Desdemona;
    Mariana of the Moated Grange.

Up this valley to the fair and market
    When young farmers from the southward ride,
Oft they linger at a sound of chanting
    In the meadows by the turnpike side;
        Long they listen,
    Deep in fancies of a fairy bride.
The Atlantic Monthly   Sarah N. Cleghorn

24   *The Interpreter*

IN the very early morning when the light was low,
    She got all ready and she went like snow,
Like snow in the springtime on a sunny hill,
And we were only frightened and can't think still.

We can't think quite that the katydids and frogs
And the little cheeping chickens and the little grunting hogs,
And the other living things that she spoke for to us
Have nothing more to tell her since it happened thus.

She never is around for anyone to touch,
But of ecstasy and longing she too knew much. . . .
And always when anyone has time to call his own
She will come and be beside him as quiet as a stone.
Contemporary Verse   Orrick Johns

25　　　　　*The Look*

STREPHON kissed me in the spring,
　　Robin in the fall,
But Colin only looked at me
　　And never kissed at all.

Strephon's kiss was lost in jest,
　　Robin's lost in play,
But the kiss in Colin's eyes
　　Haunts me night and day.

Harper's Magazine　　　　　　　　Sara Teasdale

26　　　　　*"Immortal Love"*

I

O THOU who clothest thyself in mystic form, —
　　Color, and gleam, and lonely distances;
　Whose seat the majesty of ocean is,
Shot o'er with motions of the skyey storm!
Thou with whose mortal breath the soul doth warm
　　Her being, soaring to eternal bliss;
　　Whose revelation unto us is this
Dilated world, starred with its golden swarm!

Thee rather in myself than heaven's vast light
　　Flooding the daybreak, better I discern;
The glorious morning makes all nature bright,
　　But in the soul doth riot more, and burn;
A thousand beauties rush upon my sight,
　　But to the greater light within I turn.

II

I know not who thou art to whom I pray,
    Or that indeed thou art, apart from me;
    A dweller in a lone eternity,
Or a participant of my sad way.
I only know that at the fall of day
    Fain would I in thy world companion thee;
    Upon the mystery of thy breast to be
Unconscious, and within thy love to stay.

I lose thee in the largeness when I think;
    And when again I feel, I find thee nigh;
The more my mind goes out to nature's brink,
    The more thou art removèd like the sky;
But when concentrated in love I sink,
    Thou art my nucleus; there I live and die.

III

Immortal Love, too high for my possessing, —
    Yet, lower than thee, where shall I find repose?
    Long in my youth I sang the morning rose,
By earthly things the heavenly pattern guessing!
Long fared I on, beauty and love caressing,
    And finding in my heart a place for those
    Eternal fugitives; the golden close
Of evening folds me, still their sweetness blessing.

O happy we, the first-born heirs of nature,
    For whom the Heavenly Sun delays his light!

He by the sweets of every mortal creature
  Tempers eternal beauty to our sight;
And by the glow upon love's earthly feature
  Maketh the path of our departure bright.
Scribner's Magazine   George Edward Woodberry

27   *Peter Quince at the Clavier*

I

JUST as my fingers on these keys
  Make music, so the self-same sounds
On my spirit make a music, too.

Music is feeling, then, not sound;
And thus it is that what I feel,
Here in this room, desiring you,

Thinking of your blue-shadowed silk,
Is music. It is like the strain
Waked in the elders by Susanna:

Of a green evening, clear and warm,
She bathed in her still garden, while
The red-eyed elders, watching, felt

The basses of their beings throb
In witching chords, and their thin blood
Pulse pizzicati of Hosanna.

II

In the green water, clear and warm,
Susanna lay.

She searched
The touch of Springs,
And found
Concealed imaginings.
She sighed,
For so much melody.

Upon the bank, she stood
In the cool
Of spent emotions.
She felt, among the leaves,
The dew
Of old devotions.

She walked upon the grass,
Still quavering.
The winds were like her maids,
On timid feet,
Fetching her woven scarves,
Yet wavering.

A breath upon her hand
Muted the night.
She turned —
A cymbal crashed,
And roaring horns.

III

Soon, with a noise like tambourines,
Came her attendant Byzantines.

They wondered why Susanna cried
Against the elders by her side;

And as they whispered, the refrain
Was like a willow swept by rain.

Anon, their lamps' uplifted flame
Revealed Susanna and her shame.

And then, the simpering Byzantines,
Fled, with a noise like tambourines.

IV

Beauty is momentary in the mind —
The fitful tracing of a portal;
But in the flesh it is immortal.

The body dies; the body's beauty lives,
So evenings die, in their green going,
A wave, interminably flowing.
So gardens die, their meek breath scenting
The cowl of Winter, done repenting.
So maidens die, to the auroral
Celebration of a maiden's choral.

Susanna's music touched the bawdy strings
Of those white elders; but, escaping,
Left only Death's ironic scraping.

Now, in its immortality, it plays
On the clear viol of her memory,
And makes a constant sacrament of praise.

Others: A Magazine of the New Verse

Wallace Stevens

28 *The Unknown Beloved*

I DREAMED I passed a doorway
   Where for a sign of death
White ribbons one was binding
   About a flowery wreath.

What drew me so I knew not,
   But drawing near I said,
"Kind sir, and will you tell me
   Who is it here lies dead?"

Said he, "Your most beloved
   Died here this very day,
That had known twenty Aprils
   Had she but lived till May."

Astonished I made answer,
   "Good sir, how say you so!
Here have I no beloved,
   This house I do not know."

Quoth he, "Who from the world's end
   Was destined unto thee
Here lies, thy true beloved,
   Whom thou shalt never see."

I dreamed I passed a doorway
   Where for a sign of death
White ribbons one was binding
   About a flowery wreath.

The Lyric   *John Hall Wheelock*

29 *Patterns*

I WALK down the garden paths,
And all the daffodils
Are blowing, and the bright blue squills.
I walk down the patterned garden paths
In my stiff, brocaded gown.
With my powdered hair and jewelled fan,
I too am a rare
Pattern. As I wander down
The garden paths.

My dress is richly figured,
And the train
Makes a pink and silver stain
On the gravel, and the thrift
Of the borders.
Just a plate of current fashion,
Tripping by in high-heeled, ribboned shoes.
Not a softness anywhere about me,
Only a whale-bone and brocade.
And I sink on a seat in the shade
Of a lime tree. For my passion
Wars against the stiff brocade.
The daffodils and squills
Flutter in the breeze
As they please.
And I weep;
For the lime tree is in blossom
And one small flower has dropped upon my bosom.

And the splashing of waterdrops
In the marble fountain
Comes down the garden paths.
The dripping never stops.
Underneath my stiffened gown
Is the softness of a woman bathing in a marble basin,
A basin in the midst of hedges grown
So thick, she cannot see her lover hiding,
But she guesses he is near,
And the sliding of the water
Seems the stroking of a dear
Hand upon her.
What is Summer in a fine brocaded gown!
I should like to see it lying in a heap upon the ground.
All the pink and silver crumpled up on the ground.

I would be the pink and silver as I ran along the paths,
And he would stumble after,
Bewildered by my laughter.
I should see the sun flashing from his sword hilt and the buckles on his shoes.
I would choose
To lead him in a maze along the patterned paths,
A bright and laughing maze for my heavy-booted lover,
Till he caught me in the shade,
And the buttons of his waistcoat bruised my body as he clasped me,
Aching, melting, unafraid.
With the shadows of the leaves and the sundrops,
And the plopping of the waterdrops,
All about us in the open afternoon —
I am very like to swoon

With the weight of this brocade,
For the sun sifts through the shade.

Underneath the fallen blossom
In my bosom,
Is a letter I have hid.
It was brought to me this morning by a rider from the
    Duke.
"Madam, we regret to inform you that Lord Hartwell
Died in action Thursday sen'night."
As I read it in the white morning sunlight,
The letters squirmed like snakes.
"Any answer, Madam," said my footman.
"No," I told him.
"See that the messenger takes some refreshment.
No, no answer."
And I walked into the garden,
Up and down the patterned paths,
In my stiff, correct brocade.
The blue and yellow flowers stood up proudly in the sun,
Each one.
I stood upright too,
Held rigid to the pattern
By the stiffness of my gown.
Up and down I walked,
Up and down.

In a month he would have been my husband.
In a month, here, underneath this lime,
We would have broken the pattern;
He for me, and I for him,
He as Colonel, I as lady,

On this shady seat.
He had a whim
That sunlight carried blessing.
And I answered, "It shall be as you have said."
Now he is dead.

In Summer and in Winter I shall walk
Up and down
The patterned garden paths
In my stiff, brocaded gown.
The squills and daffodils
Will give place to pillared roses, and to asters, and to snow.
I shall go
Up and down,
In my gown.
Gorgeously arrayed,
Boned and stayed.
And the softness of my body will be guarded from embrace
By each button, hook, and lace.
For the man who should loose me is dead,
Fighting with the Duke in Flanders,
In a pattern called a war.
Christ! What are patterns for?
   The Little Review   *Amy Lowell*

30   *Evensong*

    This song is of no importance,
    I will only improvise;
    Yet, maybe, here and there,
    Suddenly from these sounds a chord will start
    And piercingly touch my heart.

I

IN the pale mauve twilight, streaked with orange,
Exquisitely sweet, —
She leaned upon her balcony and looked across the street;
And across the huddled roofs of the misty city,
Across the hills of tenements, so gray,
She looked into the west with a young and infinite pity,
With a young and wistful pity, as if to say
The dark was coming, and irresistible night,
Which man would attempt to meet
With here and there a little flickering light. . . .
The orange faded, the housetops all were black,
And a strange and beautiful quiet
Came unexpected, came exquisitely sweet,
On market-place and street;
And where were lately crowds and sounds and riot
Was a gentle blowing of wind, a murmur of leaves,
A single step, or voice, and under the eaves
The scrambling of sparrows; and then the hush swept back.

II

She leaned upon her balcony, in the darkness,
Folding her hands beneath her chin;
And watched the lamps begin
Here and there to pierce like eyes the darkness, —
From windows, luminous rooms,
And from the damp dark street
Between the moving branches, and the leaves with rain
    still sweet.
It was strange: the leaves thus seen,

With the lamplight's cold bright glare thrown up among
    them, —
The restless maple leaves,
Twinkling their myriad shadows beneath the eaves, —
Were lovelier, almost, than with sunlight on them,
So bright they were with young translucent green;
Were lovelier, almost, than with moonlight on them. . . .
And looking so wistfully across the city,
With such a young, and wise, and infinite pity
For the girl who had no lover
To walk with her along a street like this,
With slow steps in the rain, both aching for a kiss, —
It seemed as if all evenings were the same,
As if all evenings came
With just such tragic peacefulness as this;
With just such hint of loneliness or pain,
The quiet after rain.

III

Would her lover, then, grow old sooner than she,
And find a night like this too damp to walk?
Would he prefer to stay indoors and talk,
Or read the evening paper, while she sewed, or darned a
    sock,
And listened to the ticking of the clock:
Would he prefer it to lamplight on a tree?
Would he be old and tired,
And, having all the comforts he desired,
Take no interest in the twilight coming down
So beautifully and quietly on the town?
Would her lover, then, grow old sooner than she?

IV

A neighbor started singing, singing a child to sleep.
It was strange: a song thus heard, —
In the misty evening, after an afternoon of rain, —
Seemed more beautiful than happiness, more beautiful than pain,
Seemed to escape the music and the word,
Only, somehow, to keep
A warmth that was lovelier than the song of any bird.
Was it because it came up through this tree,
Through the lucent leaves that twinkled on this tree,
With the bright lamp there beneath them in the street?
It was exquisitely sweet:
So unaffected, so unconscious that it was heard.
Or was it because she looked across the city,
Across the hills of tenements, so black,
And thought of all the mothers with a young and infinite pity? . . .
The child had fallen asleep, the hush swept back,
The leaves hung lifeless on the tree.

V

It was too bad the sky was dark..
A cat came slinking close along the wall.
For the moon was full just now, and in the park,
If the sky were clear at all,
The lovers upon the moonlight grass would sprawl,
And whisper in the shadows, and laugh, and there
She would be going, maybe, with a white rose in her hair . . .
But would youth at last grow weary of these things,

Of the ribbons and the laces,
And the latest way of putting up one's hair?
Would she no longer care,
In that undiscovered future of recurring springs,
If, growing old and plain, she no longer turned the faces
And saw the people stare?
Would she hear music and not yearn
To take her lover's arm for one more turn? . . .
The leaves hung breathless on the dripping maple tree,
The man across the street was going out.
It was the evening made her think such things, no doubt.
But would her lover grow old sooner than she? . . .
Only the evening made her think such things, no doubt. . . .

VI

And yet, and yet, —
Seeing the tired city, and the trees so still and wet, —
It seemed as if all evenings were the same;
As if all evenings came,
Despite her smile at thinking of a kiss,
With just such tragic peacefulness as this;
With just such hint of loneliness or pain;
The perfect quiet that comes after rain.
   The Poetry Review of America   *Conrad Aiken*

31   *Waiting*

I THOUGHT my heart would break
  Because the Spring was slow.
I said, "How long young April sleeps
  Beneath the snow!"

But when at last she came,
And buds broke in the dew,
I dreamed of my lost love,
And my heart broke, too!

Harper's Magazine   *Charles Hanson Towne*

32   *The Broken Field*

MY soul is a dark ploughed field
   In the cold rain;
My soul is a broken field
   Ploughed by pain.

Where windy grass and flowers
   Were growing,
The field lies broken now
   For another sowing.

Great Sower, when you tread
   My field again,
Scatter the furrows there
   With better grain.

The Yale Review   *Sara Teasdale*

33 *"Grandmither, Think not I Forget"*

GRANDMITHER, think not I forget, when I come back to town,
An' wander the old ways again an' tread them up an' down.
I never smell the clover bloom, nor see the swallows pass,
Without I mind how good ye were unto a little lass.

I never hear the winter rain a-pelting all night through,
Without I think and mind me of how cold it falls on you.
And if I come not often to your bed beneath the thyme,
Mayhap 't is that I'd change wi' ye, and gie my bed for thine,
    Would like to sleep in thine.

I never hear the summer winds among the roses blow,
Without I wonder why it was ye loved the lassie so.
Ye gave me cakes and lollipops and pretty toys a score, —
I never thought I should come back and ask ye now for more.
Grandmither, gie me your still, white hands, that lie upon your breast,
For mine do beat the dark all night and never find me rest;
They grope among the shadows an' they beat the cold black air,
They go seekin' in the darkness, an' they never find him there,
    As They never find him there.

Grandmither, gie me your sightless eyes, that I may never see
His own a-burnin' full o' love that must not shine for me.
Grandmither, gie me your peaceful lips, white as the kirkyard snow,
For mine be red wi' burnin' thirst an' he must never know.
Grandmither, gie me your clay-stopped ears, that I may never hear
My lad a-singin' in the night when I am sick wi' fear;
A-singing when the moonlight over a' the land is white —
Aw God! I'll up an' go to him a-singin' in the night,
    A-callin' in the night.

Grandmither, gie me your clay-cold heart that has forgot
  to ache
For mine be fire within my breast and yet it cannot
  break.
It beats an' throbs forever for the things that must not
  be,—
An' can ye not let me creep in an' rest awhile by ye?
A little lass afeard o' dark slept by ye years agone —
Ah, she has found what night can hold 'twixt sunset an'
  the dawn!
So when I plant the rose an' rue above your grave for ye,
Ye'll know it's under rue an' rose that I would like to be,
  That I would like to be.
  McClure's Magazine　　　　　　　*Willa Sibert Cather*

34　　*Hungarian Love-Lament*

THEY say the cranes last night did cry
　　　Overhead.
　　I did not hear them,
For in a hut by Tisza's torrents
　　My love lies dead.
I heard the whinny of her milk-white steed
　　Calling to her,
　　That heard I.
They say the oak-tree's leaves are sere —
　　What care I?
I have some faded violets;
　　Those I hold dear —
　　She gave them me.

They say that Szolnok's field 's afire;
    If so, I care not.
That could not keep me from my love
    Were she not cold.
    Saw'st Szolnok's flames?
Oh, well, they could not warm me;
    My blood is chilled.
They say three gypsies at the tavern
    Sang their songs.
    Let them sing!
    I could not dance —
I am too lonely for their minstrelsy.
    I wish my love might waken,
    But she cannot.
Fresh violets she would bring me,
    But she will not.
For cold in death she lies, by Tisza's torrents,
    And she'll not come again!
    She cannot.
Let the wild cranes cry, far and high,
    Overhead.

Lippincott's Magazine   Ethel Syford

35   Old Fairingdown

SOFT as a treader on mosses
    I go through the village that sleeps;
The village too early abed,
For the night still shuffles, a gypsy,
In the woods of the east,
And the west remembers the sun.

Not all are asleep; there are faces
That lean from the walls of the gardens.
Look sharply, or you will not see them,
Or think them another stone in the wall.
I spoke to a stone, and it answered
Like an agèd rock that crumbles
Each falling piece was a word.
"Five have I buried," it said,
"And seven are over the sea."

Here is a hut that I pass,
So lowly it has no brow,
And dwarfs sit within at a table.
A boy waits apart by the hearth;
On his face is the patience of firelight,
But his eyes seek the door and a far-world.
It is not the call to the table he waits,
But the call of the sea-rimmed forests,
And cities that stir in a dream.
I haste by the low-browed door,
Lest my arms go in and betray me,
A mother jealously passing.
He will go, the pale dwarf, and walk tall among giants;
The child with his eyes on the far land,
And fame like a young curled leaf in his heart.

The stream that darts from the hanging hill
Like a silver wing that must sing as it flies,
Is folded and still on the breast
Of the village that sleeps.
Each mute old house is more old than the other,
And each wears its vines like ragged hair

Round the half-blind windows.
If a child should laugh, if a girl should sing,
Would the houses rub the vines from their eyes,
And listen and live?
A voice comes now from a cottage,
A voice that is young and must sing,
A honeyed stab on the air,
And the houses do not wake.

I look through the leaf-blowsed window,
And start as a gazer who, passing a death-vault,
Sees Life sitting hopeful within.
She is young, but a woman, round-breasted,
Waiting the peril of Eve;
And she makes the shadows about her sweet
As the glooms that play in a pine-wood.
She sits at a harpsichord (old as the walls are),
And longing flows in the trickling, fairy notes
Like a hidden brook in a forest
Seeking and seeking the sun.

I have watched a young tree on the edge of a wood
When the mist is weaving and drifting;
Slowly the boughs disappear, and the leaves reach out
Like the drowning hands of children,
Till a grey blur quivers cold
Where the green grace drank of the sun.
So now, as I gaze, the morrows
Creep weaving and winding their mist
Round the beauty of her who sings.
They hide the soft rings of her hair,
Dear as a child's curling fingers;

OF MAGAZINE VERSE

They shut out the trembling sun of eyes
That are deep as a bending mother's;
And her bridal body is scarfed with their chill.

For old, and old, is the story;
Over and over I hear it,
Over and over I listen to murmurs
That are always the same in these towns that sleep;
Where, grey and unwed, a woman passes,
Her cramped, drab gown the bounds of a world
She holds with grief and silence;
And a gossip whose tongue alone is unwithered
Mumbles the tale by her affable gate;
How the lad must go, and the girl must stay,
Singing alone to the years and a dream;
Then a letter, a rumor, a word,
From the land that reaches for lovers
And gives them not back;
And the maiden looks up with a face that is old;
Her smile, as her body, is evermore barren;
Her cheek like the bark of the beech-tree
Where climbs the grey winter.

Now have I seen her young,
The lone girl singing,
With the full, round breast and the berry lip,
And heart that runs to a dawn-rise
On new-world mountains.
The weeping ash in the dooryard
Gathers the song in its boughs,
And the gown of dawn she will never wear.

I can listen no more; good-by, little town, old Fairingdown.
I climb the long, dark hill side,
But the ache I have found here I cannot outclimb.
O Heart, if we had not heard, if we did not know
There is that in the village that never will sleep!

   Hampshire, England.
   Scribner's Magazine   *Olive Tilford Dargan*

36   *Motherhood*

MARY, the Christ long slain, passed silently,
    Following the children joyously astir
Under the cedrus and the olive-tree,
Pausing to let their laughter float to her.
Each voice an echo of a voice more dear,
She saw a little Christ in every face;
When lo, another woman, gliding near,
Yearned o'er the tender life that filled the place.
And Mary sought the woman's hand, and spoke:
"I know thee not, yet know thy memory tossed
With all a thousand dreams their eyes evoke
Who bring to thee a child beloved and lost.

   "I, too, have rocked my little one,
     O, He was fair!
   Yea, fairer than the fairest sun,
   And like its rays through amber spun
     His sun-bright hair.
   Still I can see it shine and shine."
   "Even so," the woman said, "was mine."

"His ways were ever darling ways," —
And Mary smiled, —
"So soft, so clinging! Glad relays
Of love were all His precious days.
My little child!
My infinite star! My music fled!"
"Even so was mine," the woman said.

Then whispered Mary: "Tell me, thou,
Of thine." And she:
"O, mine was rosy as a bough
Blooming with roses, sent, somehow,
To bloom for me!
His balmy fingers left a thrill
Within my breast that warms me still."

Then gazed she down some wilder, darker hour,
And said, when Mary questioned, knowing not:
"Who art thou, mother of so sweet a flower?"
"I am the mother of Iscariot."
The North American Review   *Agnes Lee*

The Hill Wife

LONELINESS

(Her Word)

ONE ought not to have to care
   So much as you and I
Care when the birds come round the house
   To seem to say good-bye;

Or care so much when they come back
　　With whatever it is they sing;
The truth being we are as much
　　Too glad for the one thing

As we are too sad for the other here —
　　With birds that fill their breasts
But with each other and themselves
　　And their built or driven nests.

HOUSE FEAR

Always — I tell you this they learned —
Always at night when they returned
To the lonely house from far away
To lamps unlighted and fire gone gray,
They learned to rattle the lock and key
To give whatever might chance to be
Warning and time to be off in flight:
And preferring the out- to the in-door night,
They learned to leave the house-door wide
Until they had lit the lamp inside.

THE SMILE

(Her Word)

I did n't like the way he went away.
That smile! It never came of being gay.
Still he smiled — did you see him? — I was sure!
Perhaps because we gave him only bread
And the wretch knew from that that we were poor.
Perhaps because he let us give instead

Of seizing from us as he might have seized.
Perhaps he mocked at us for being wed,
Or being very young (and he was pleased)
To have a vision of us old and dead).
I wonder how far down the road he's got.
He's watching from the woods as like as not.

THE OFT-REPEATED DREAM

She had no saying dark enough
　For the dark pine that kept
Forever trying the window-latch
　Of the room where they slept.

The tireless but ineffectual hands
　That with every futile pass
Made the great tree seem as a little bird
　Before the mystery of glass!

It never had been inside the room,
　And only one of the two
Was afraid in an oft-repeated dream
　Of what the tree might do.

THE IMPULSE

It was too lonely for her there,
　And too wild,
And since there were but two of them,
　And no child,

And work was little in the house,
　She was free,
And followed where he furrowed field,
　Or felled tree.

She rested on a log and tossed
    The fresh chips,
With a song only to herself
    On her lips.

And once she went to break a bough
    Of black alder.
She strayed so far she scarcely heard
    When he called her —

And did n't answer — did n't speak —
    Or return.
She stood, and then she ran and hid
    In the fern.

He never found her, though he looked
    Everywhere,
And he asked at her mother's house
    Was she there.

Sudden and swift and light as that
    The ties gave,
And he learned of finalities
    Beside the grave.

The Yale Review   Robert Frost

38 *The Wife*

HE sees the wife, from slim young comeliness,
    With bearing of his children and their care,
Grow stooped and withered, and the shining hair
That was his pride grow thin and lustreless;

Day after day, with wordless, pained distress,
He strives to ease the load her shoulders bear,
Lifting a burden here, a burden there,
Or offering some clumsy, rare caress.

But ah! her girl-face never was so fair,
And eyes and lips that answered his desire,
Are limned with sacred meaning to him now;
To his rapt sight, an angel might aspire
To claim the stature of her soul, or wear
The halo that surrounds her mother-brow.

The Delineator   *Anna Spencer Twitchell*

39   *Needle Travel*

I SIT at home and sew,
I ply my needle and thread,
But the trip around the garment's hem
Is not the path I tread;
My stitches neat,
With their rhythmic beat,
Keep time to very different feet,
On a different journey sped.

Now, glad heart
Tip-toe, tip-toe,
They must not hear you,
They must not know,
They must not follow where you go.

Bare, brown feet on the dusty road,
Unbound body free of its load,
Limbs that need no stinging goad
Step, step out on the dusty road.

Friends to greet on the jolly road,
Lopeing rabbit, and squatting toad,
Beetle, trundling along with your load;
Hey, little friends,
Good-day, good-morrow,
You see me to-day,
You forget me to-morrow.

Time to chase you across the road,
Lopeing rabbit, and poke you, toad,
Upset you, beetle with your load;
Hey, little friends,
Good-day.

Bare, brown feet in the shelving pool,
Unbound body, relaxed and cool,
Limbs lying bare and beautiful;
Hey, green pool,
Good-day, good-morrow,
You hold me to-day,
You forget me to-morrow.

Time to float in you, rapt and cool,
Swim the rapids above you, pool,
Dive in your waters bountiful;
Hey, sweet friend,
Good-day.

I sit at home and sew,
I ply my needle and thread,
But the trip around the garment's hem
Is not the path I tread.
The Masses   Margaret French Patton

40   *Cradle Song*

I

LORD GABRIEL, wilt thou not rejoice
When at last a little boy's
  Cheek lies heavy as a rose,
    And his eyelids close?

Gabriel, when that hush may be,
This sweet hand all heedfully
  I'll undo, for thee alone,
    From his mother's own.

Then the far blue highways paven
With the burning stars of heaven
  He shall gladden with the sweet
    Hasting of his feet —

Feet so brightly bare and cool,
Leaping, as from pool to pool;
  From a little laughing boy
    Splashing rainbow joy!

Gabriel, wilt thou understand
How to keep his hovering hand? —
  Never shut, as in a bond
    From the bright beyond? —

Nay, but though it cling and close
Tightly as a climbing rose,
  Clasp it only so, — aright,
    Lest his heart take fright.

    (Dormi, dormi, tu:
    The dusk is hung with blue.)

II

Lord Michael, wilt not thou rejoice
When at last a little boy's
  Heart, a shut-in murmuring bee,
    Turns him unto thee?

Wilt thou heed thine armor well, —
To take his hand from Gabriel
  So his radiant cup of dream
    May not spill a gleam?

He will take thy heart in thrall,
Telling o'er thy breastplate, all
  Colors, in his bubbling speech,
    With his hand to each.

    (Dormi, dormi tu.
    Sapphire is the blue;
    Pearl and beryl, they are called,
    Chrysoprase and emerald,
    Sard and amethyst.
      Numbered so, and kissed.)

Ah, but find some angel word
For thy sharp, subduing sword!
  Yea, Lord Michael, make no doubt
    He will find it out:

    (Dormi, dormi tu!)
    His eyes will look at you.

III

Last, a little morning space,
Lead him to that leafy place
  Where Our Lady sits awake,
    For all mothers' sake.

Bosomed with the Blessèd One,
He shall mind her of her Son,
  Once so folded from all harms,
    In her shrining arms.

    (In her veil of blue,
    Dormi, dormi tu.)

  So; — and fare thee well. —
  Softly, — Gabriel . . .
When the first faint red shall come,
Bid the Day-star lead him home,
  For the bright World's sake, —
    To my heart, awake.

Scribner's Magazine   *Josephine Preston Peabody*

41   The Bacchante to her Babe

Scherzo

COME, sprite, and dance! The sun is up,
The wind runs laughing down the sky
That brims with morning like a cup.
Sprite, we must race him,
We must chase him —
You and I!
And skim across the fuzzy heather —
You and joy and I together
Whirling by!

    You merry little roll of fat! —
Made warm to kiss, and smooth to pat,
And round to toy with, like a cub;
To put one's nozzle in and rub
And breathe you in like breath of kine,
Like juice of vine,
That sets my morning heart a-tingling,
Dancing, jingling,
All the glad abandon mingling
Of wind and wine!

    Sprite, you are love, and you are joy,
A happiness, a dream, a toy,
A god to laugh with,
Love to chaff with,
The sun come down in tangled gold,
The moon to kiss, and spring to hold.

There was a time once, long ago,
Long — oh, long since . . . I scarcely know.
Almost I had forgot . . .
There was a time when you were not,
You merry sprite, save as a strain,
The strange dull pain
Of green buds swelling
In warm, straight dwelling
That must burst to the April rain.
A little heavy I was then
And dull — and glad to rest.   And when
The travail came
In searing flame . . .
But, sprite, that was so long ago! —
A century! — I scarcely know.
Almost I had forgot
When you were not.

So, little sprite, come dance with me!
The sun is up, the wind is free!
Come now and trip it,
Romp and skip it,
Earth is young and so are we.
Sprite, you and I will dance together
On the heather,
Glad with all the procreant earth,
With all the fruitage of the trees,
And golden pollen on the breeze,
With plants that bring the grain to birth,
With beast and bird,
Feathered and furred,
With youth and hope and life and love,

And joy thereof —
While we are part of all, we two —
For my glad burgeoning in you!

    So, merry little roll of fat,
Made warm to kiss and smooth to pat
And round to toy with, like a cub,
To put one's nozzle in and rub,
My god to laugh with,
Love to chaff with,
Come and dance beneath the sky,
You and I!
Look out with those round wondering eyes,
And squirm, and gurgle — and grow wise!

Poetry: A Magazine of Verse   Eunice Tietjens

42   *The Son*

(*Southern Ohio Market Town*)

I HEARD an old farm-wife,
   Selling some barley,
Mingle her life with life
   And the name "Charley."

Saying: "The crop's all in,
   We're about through now;
Long nights will soon begin,
   We're just us two now.

"Twelve bushel at sixty cents,
  It's all I carried —
He sickened making fence;
  He was to be married —

"It feels like frost was near —
  His hair was curly.
The spring was late that year,
  But the harvest early."

The New Republic   *Ridgely Torrence*

43   *With Cassock Black, Baret and Book*

WITH cassock black, baret and book,
  Father Saran goes by;
I think he goes to say a prayer
  For one who has to die.

Even so, some day, Father Saran
  May say a prayer for me;
Myself meanwhile, the Sister tells,
  Should pray unceasingly.

They kneel who pray: how may I kneel
  Who face to ceiling lie,
Shut out by all that man has made
  From God who made the sky?

They lift who pray — the low earth-born —
  A humble heart to God:
But O, my heart of clay is proud —
  True sister to the sod.

I look into the face of God,
   They say bends over me;
I search the dark, dark face of God —
   O what is it I see?

I see — who lie fast bound, who may
   Not kneel, who can but seek —
I see mine own face over me,
   With tears upon its cheek.

The Atlantic Monthly   Grace Fallow Norton

44   Moods

I

AN ASTRONOMER

ON a lone hillside
   A Navajo shepherd
Wrapt in his blanket,
Hugged his knees,
Dreamed into the night —
A wisp of a crescent,
A sky full of stars —
In his thought
He was asking:
"Do my lanterns
Shine up to the stars?"

II

A VASE OF CHINESE IVORY

   In the museum
   It had no name:

OF MAGAZINE VERSE

It was only the life work
Of one almond-eyed heathen —
Just one of a million!
Look closer
And you will see
A soul,
Unique and beautiful.

III
MESSAGES

He plodded along
The deep-rutted road,
The old farmer,
Face as red as sumach,
Wind-colored;
Happy.

The bee-drone hum
Of wires overhead
Was song and laughter to him,
Yet the wires were laden
With messages of strife, and sorrow, and sin.

IV
THE HEIGHTS

Alone,
On a high mountain trail,
I drew strength from the sky;
My thoughts went out
Like my shadow at sunset:
I grew great as my shadow at sunset.

73

V

SOLITUDE

Youth!
If there be madness
In your soul,
Go to the mountain solitudes
Where you can grow up
To your madness.

The Little Review   *David O' Neil*

45   *Cinquains*

I

TRIAD

THESE be
   Three silent things:
The falling snow . . . the hour
Before the dawn . . . the mouth of one
Just dead.

II

MOON-SHADOWS

Still as
On windless nights
The moon-cast shadows are,
So still will be my heart when I
Am dead.

III

SUSANNA AND THE ELDERS

"Why do
You thus devise
Evil against her?" "For that
She is beautiful, delicate;
Therefore."

IV

NIGHT WINDS

The old
Old winds that blew
When chaos was, what do
They tell the clattered trees that I
Should weep?

V

AMAZE

I know
Not these hands
And yet I think there was
A woman like me once had hands
Like these.

VI

THE WARNING

Just now,
Out of the strange
Still dusk ... as strange, as still ...
A white moth flew. ... Why am I grown
So cold?

Others: A Magazine of the New Verse

Adelaide Crapsey

46   *The Regents' Examination*

MUFFLED sounds of the city climbing to me at the window,
Here in the summer noon-tide students busily writing,
Children of quaint-clad immigrants, fresh from the hut and the Ghetto,
Writing of pious Æneas and funeral rites of Anchises.
Old-World credo and custom, alien accents and features,
Plunged in the free-school hopper, grist for the Anglo-Saxons —
Old-World sweetness and light, and fiery struggle of heroes,
Flashed on the blinking peasants, dull with the grime of their bondage!
Race that are infant in knowledge, ancient in grief and traditions —
Lore that is tranquil with age and starry with gleams of the future —
What is the thing that will come from the might of the elements blending?
Neuter and safe shall it be? Or a flame to burst us asunder?
   Scribner's Magazine   Jessie Wallace Hughan

47   *Train-Mates*

OUTSIDE hove Shasta, snowy height on height,
   A glory; but a negligible sight,
For you had often seen a mountain-peak
But not my paper. So we came to speak. . .

OF MAGAZINE VERSE

A smoke, a smile, — a good way to commence
The comfortable exchange of difference! —
You a young engineer, five feet eleven,
Forty-five chest, with football in your heaven,
Liking a road-bed newly built and clean,
Your fingers hot to cut away the green
Of brush and flowers that bring beside a track
The kind of beauty steel lines ought to lack, —
And I a poet, wistful of my betters,
Reading George Meredith's high-hearted letters,
Joining betweenwhile in the mingled speech
Of a drummer, circus-man, and parson, each
Absorbing to himself — as I to me
And you to you — a glad identity!

After a time, when the others went away,
A curious kinship made us choose to stay,
Which I could tell you now; but at the time
You thought of baseball teams and I of rhyme,
Until we found that we were college men
And smoked more easily and smiled again;
And I from Cambridge cried, the poet still:
"I know your fine Greek Theatre on the hill
At Berkeley!" With your happy Grecian head
Upraised, "I never saw the place," you said.
"Once I was free of class, I always went
Out to the field."
    Young engineer, you meant
As fair a tribute to the better part
As ever I did. Beauty of the heart
Is evident in temples. But it breathes
Alive where athletes quicken curly wreaths,

Which are the lovelier because they die.
You are a poet quite as much as I,
Though differences appear in what we do,
And I am athlete quite as much as you.
Because you half-surmised my quarter-mile
And I your quatrain, we could greet and smile.
Who knows but we shall look again and find
The circus-man and drummer, not behind
But leading in our visible estate,
As discus-thrower and as laureate?
The Yale Review   *Witter Bynner*

48   Thanksgiving for our Task

THE sickle is dulled of the reaping and the threshing-
    floor is bare;
The dust of night's in the air.
The peace of the weary is ours:
All day we have taken the fruit and the grain and the
    seeds of the flowers.

The ev'ning is chill,
It is good now to gather in peace by the flames of the fire.
We have done now the deed that we did for our need and
    desire:
We have wrought our will.

And now for the boon of abundance and golden increase,
And immurèd peace,
Shall we thank our God?
Bethink us, amid His indulgence, His terrible rod?

Shall we be as the maple and oak,
Strew the earth with our gold, giving only bare boughs to
  the sky?
Nay, the pine stayeth green while the Winter growls
  sullenly by,
And doth not revoke

For soft days or stern days the pledge of its constancy.
Shall we not be
Also the same through all days,
Giving thanks when the battle breaks on us, in toil giving
  praise?

O Father who saw at the dawn,
That the folly of Pride would be the lush weed of our
  sin,
There is better than that in our hearts, O enter therein,
A light burneth, though wan

And weak be the flame, yet it gloweth, our Humility!
Ah, how can it be
Trimmed o' the wick,
And replenished with oil to burn brightly and golden and
  quick?

For deep in our hearts
We wish to be thankful through lean years and fat without change,
Knowing that here Thou hast set for the spirit a range:
We would play well our parts,

Making America throb with the building of souls and the
  glory of good;
Yea, and we would,

And before the last Autumn we will
Build a temple from ocean to ocean where deeds never
    still

Melodiously shall proclaim
Thanksgiving forever that Thou hast set here to our hand
So wondrous a mystical harvest, that Thou dost demand
Sheaves bound in Thy name,

Yea, supersubstantial sheaves of strong souls that have
    grown
Fain to be known
As the corn of Thine occident field:
O Yielder of All, can America worthily thank Thee till
    such be her yield?

In the mellowing light
Of the goldenest days that precede the gray days of the
    year,
We sing Thee our harvesting song and we pray Thee to
    hear,
In the midst of Thy might:

> Labor is given to us,
>   Let us give thanks!
> Power worketh through us,
>   Let us give thanks!
> Not for what we have
> (So might speak a slave),
> Not for the garnering,
> Gratefully we sing,
> But for the mighty thing
> We must do, travailing!

For our task and for our strength;
For the journey and its length;
For our dauntless eagerness;
For our humbling weariness;
For these, for these, O Father,
   Let us give thanks!
For these, O Mighty Father,
   Take Thou our thanks!

The Forum   *Shaemas O Sheel*

49   *School*

I

OLD Hezekiah leaned hard on his hoe
   And squinted long at Eben, his lank son.
The silence shrilled with crickets. Day was done,
    And, row on dusky row,
Tall bean poles ribbed with dark the gold-bright afterglow.
Eben stood staring: ever, one by one,
The tendril tops turned ashen as they flared.
    Still Eben stared.

Oh, there is wonder on New Hampshire hills,
Hoeing the warm bright furrows of brown earth,
And there is grandeur in the stone wall's birth,
    And in the sweat that spills
From rugged toil its sweetness; yet for wild young wills
There is no dew of wonder, but stark dearth,
In one old man who hoes his long bean rows,
    And only hoes.

Old Hezekiah turned slow on his heel.
He touched his son. — Through all the carking day
There are so many littlish cares to weigh
    Large natures down, and steel
The heart of understanding. — "Son, how is't ye
    feel?
What are ye starin' on — a gal?" A ray
Flushed Eben from the fading afterglow:
    He dropped his hoe.

He dropped his hoe, but sudden stooped again
And raised it where it fell. Nothing he spoke,
But bent his knee and *crack!* the handle broke,
    Splintering. With glare of pain,
He flung the pieces down, and stamped upon them;
    then —
Like one who leaps out naked from his cloak —
Ran. "Here, come back! Where are ye bound — you
    fool?"
    He cried — "To school!"

II

Now on the mountain Morning laughed with light —
With light and all the future in her face,
For there she looked on many a far-off-place
    And wild adventurous sight,
For which the mad young autumn wind hallooed with
    might
And dared the roaring mill-brook to the race,
Where blue-jays screamed beyond the pine-dark pool —
    "To school! — To school!"

Blackcoated, Eben took the barefoot trail,
Holding with wary hand his Sunday boots;
Harsh catbirds mocked his whistling with their hoots;
    Under his swallowtail
Against his hip-strap bumping, clinked his dinner pail;
Frost maples flamed, lone thrushes touched their lutes;
Gray squirrels bobbed, with tails stiff curved to backs,
    To eye his tracks.

Soon at the lonely crossroads he passed by
The little one-room schoolhouse. He peered in.
There stood the bench where he had often been
    Admonished flagrantly
To drone his numbers: Now to this he said good-bye
For mightier lure of more romantic scene:
Goodbye to childish rule and homely chore
    Forevermore!

All day he hastened like the flying cloud
Breathless above him, big with dreams, yet dumb.
With tightened jaw he chewed the tart spruce gum,
    And muttered half aloud
Huge oracles. At last, where through the pine-tops bowed
The sun, it rose! — His heart beat like a drum.
There, there it rose — his tower of prophecy:
    The Academy!

III

They learn to live who learn to contemplate,
For contemplation is the unconfined
God who creates us. To the growing mind
    Freedom to think is fate,

And all that age and after-knowledge augurate
Lies in a little dream of youth enshrined:
That dream to nourish with the skilful rule
    Of love — is school.

Eben, in mystic tumult of his teens,
Stood bursting — like a ripe seed — into soul.
All his life long he had watched the great hills roll
    Their shadows, tints and sheens
By sun- and moon-rise; yet the bane of hoeing beans,
And round of joyless chores, his father's toll,
Blotted their beauty; nature was as not:
    He had never *thought*.

But now he climbed his boyhood's castle tower
And knocked: Ah, well then for his after-fate
That one of nature's masters opened the gate,
    Where like an April shower
Live influence quickened all his earth-blind seed to
       power.
Strangely his sense of truth grew passionate,
And like a young bull, led in yoke to drink,
    He bowed to think.

There also bowed their heads with him to quaff —
The snorting herd! And many a wholesome grip
He had of rivalry and fellowship.
    Often the game was rough,
But Eben tossed his horns and never called it off;
For still through play and task his Dream would slip —
A radiant Herdsman, guiding destiny
    To his degree.

IV

Once more old Hezekiah stayed his hoe
To squint at Eben. Silent, Eben scanned
A little roll of sheepskin in his hand,
    While, row on dusky row,
Tall bean poles ribbed with dark the gold-bright afterglow.
The boy looked up: Here was another land!
Mountain and farm with mystic beauty flared
    Where Eben stared.

Stooping, he lifted with a furtive smile
Two splintered sticks, and spliced them. Nevermore
His spirit would go beastwise to his chore
    Blinded, for even while
He stooped to the old task, sudden in the sunset's pile
His radiant Herdsman swung a fiery door,
Through which came forth with far-borne trumpetings
    Poets and kings,

His fellow conquerors: there Virgil dreamed,
There Cæsar fought and won the barbarous tribes,
There Darwin, pensive, bore the ignorant gibes,
    And One with thorns redeemed
From malice the wild hearts of men: there flared and
    gleamed
With chemic fire the forges of old scribes,
Testing anew the crucibles of toil
    To save God's soil.

So Eben turned again to hoe his beans,
But now, to ballads which his Herdsman sung,

Henceforth he hoed the dream in with the dung,
    And for his ancient spleens
Planting new joys, imagination found him means.
At last old Hezekiah loosed his tongue:
"Well, boy, this school — what has it learned ye to know?"
    He said: "To hoe."

The Forum   Percy MacKaye

50   *Yankee Doodle*

[This poem is intended as a description of a sort of Blashfield mural painting on the sky. To be sung to the tune of "Yankee Doodle," yet in a slower, more orotund fashion. It is presumably an exercise for an entertainment on the evening of Washington's Birthday.]

DAWN this morning burned all red
    Watching them in wonder.
There I saw our spangled flag
Divide the clouds asunder.
Then there followed Washington.
Ah, he rode from glory,
Cold and mighty as his name
And stern as Freedom's story.
Unsubdued by burning dawn
Led his continentals.
Vast they were, and strange to see
In gray old regimentals: —
Marching still with bleeding feet,
Bleeding feet and jesting —
Marching from the judgment throne
With energy unresting.

OF MAGAZINE VERSE

How their merry quickstep played —
Silver, sharp, sonorous,
Piercing through with prophecy
The demons' rumbling chorus —
Behold the ancient powers of sin
And slavery before them! —
Sworn to stop the glorious dawn,
The pit-black clouds hung o'er them.
Plagues that rose to blast the day
Fiend and tiger faces,
Monsters plotting bloodshed for
The patient toiling races.
Round the dawn their cannon raged,
Hurling bolts of thunder,
Yet before our spangled flag
Their host was cut asunder.
Like a mist they fled away . . .
Ended wrath and roaring.
Still our restless soldier-host
From East to West went pouring.

High beside the sun of noon
They bore our banner splendid.
All its days of stain and shame
And heaviness were ended.
Men were swelling now the throng
From great and lowly station —
Valiant citizens to-day
Of every tribe and nation.
Not till night their rear-guard came,
Down the west went marching,
And left behind the sunset-rays

In beauty overarching.
War-god banners lead us still,
Rob, enslave and harry
Let us rather choose to-day
The flag the angels carry —
Flag we love, but brighter far —
Soul of it made splendid:
Let its days of stain and shame
And heaviness be ended.
Let its fifes fill all the sky,
Redeemed souls marching after,
Hills and mountains shake with song,
While seas roll on in laughter.

The Metropolitan Magazine   *Vachel Lindsay*

51   *Cassandra*

I HEARD one who said: "Verily,
  What word have I for children here?
Your Dollar is your only Word,
  The wrath of it your only fear.

"You built it altars tall enough
  To make you see, but you are blind;
You cannot leave it long enough
  To look before you or behind.

"When Reason beckons you to pause,
  You laugh and say that you know best;
But what it is you know, you keep
  As dark as ingots in a chest.

OF MAGAZINE VERSE

"You laugh and answer, 'We are young;
  O leave us now, and let us grow.' —
Not asking how much more of this
  Will Time endure or Fate bestow.

"Because a few complacent years
  Have made your peril of your pride,
Think you that you are to go on
  Forever pampered and untried?

"What lost eclipse of history,
  What bivouac of the marching stars,
Has given the sign for you to see
  Millenniums and last great wars?

"What unrecorded overthrow
  Of all the world has ever known,
Or ever been, has made itself
  So plain to you, and you alone?

"Your Dollar, Dove, and Eagle make
  A Trinity that even you
Rate higher than you rate yourselves;
  It pays, it flatters, and it's new.

"And though your very flesh and blood
  Be what your Eagle eats and drinks,
You'll praise him for the best of birds,
  Not knowing what the Eagle thinks.

"The power is yours, but not the sight;
  You see not upon what you tread;
You have the ages for your guide,
  But not the wisdom to be led.

"Think you to tread forever down
    The merciless old verities?
And are you never to have eyes
    To see the world for what it is?

"Are you to pay for what you have
    With all you are?" — No other word
We caught, but with a laughing crowd
    Moved on. None heeded, and few heard.
The Boston Transcript   *Edwin Arlington Robinson*

52   *The Bonfire*

"OH, let's go up the hill and scare ourselves,
    As reckless as the best of them to-night,
By setting fire to all the brush we piled
With pitchy hands to wait for rain or snow.
Oh, let's not wait for rain to make it safe.
The pile is ours: we dragged it bough on bough
Down dark converging paths between the pines.
Let's not care what we do with it to-night.
Divide it? No! But burn it as one pile
The way we piled it. And let's be the talk
Of people brought to windows by a light
Thrown from somewhere against their wall-paper.
Rouse them all, both the free and not so free
With saying what they'd like to do to us
For what they'd better wait till we have done.

Let's all but bring to life this old volcano,
If that is what the mountain ever was —
And scare ourselves. Let wild fire loose we will . . ."
"And scare you too?" the children said together.

"Why would n't it scare me to have a fire
Begin in smudge with ropy smoke and know
That still, if I repent, I may recall it,
But in a moment not: a little spurt
Of burning fatness, and then nothing but
The fire itself can put it out, and that
By burning out, and before it burns out
It will have roared first and mixed sparks with stars
And sweeping round it with a flaming sword,
Made the dim trees stand back in wider circle —
Done so much and I know not how much more
I mean it shall not do if I can bind it.
Well if it does n't with its draft bring on
A wind to blow in earnest from some quarter,
As once it did with me upon an April.
The breezes were so spent with winter blowing
They seemed to fail the bluebirds under them
Short of the perch their languid flight was toward;
And my flame made a pinnacle to heaven
As I walked once round it in possession.
But the wind out of doors — you know the saying.
There came a gust. You used to think the trees
Made wind by fanning since you never knew
It blow but that you saw the trees in motion.
Something or someone watching made that gust.
  It put that flame tip-down and dabbed the grass
  Of over-winter with the least tip-touch

Your tongue gives salt or sugar in your hand.
The place it reached to blackened instantly.
The black was all there was by day-light,
That and the merest curl of cigarette smoke —
And a flame slender as the hepaticas,
Blood-root, and violets so soon to be now.
But the black spread like black death on the ground,
And I think the sky darkened with a cloud
Like winter and evening coming on together.
There were enough things to be thought of then.
Where the field stretches toward the north
And setting sun to Hyla brook, I gave it
To flames without twice thinking, where it verges
Upon the road, to flames too, though in fear
They might find fuel there, in withered brake,
Grass its full length, old silver golden-rod,
And alder and grape vine entanglement,
To leap the dusty deadline. For my own
I took what front there was beside. I knelt
And thrust hands in and held my face away.
Fight such a fire by rubbing not by beating.
A board is the best weapon if you have it.
I had my coat. And oh, I knew, I knew,
And said out loud, I could n't bide the smother
And heat so close in; but the thought of all
The woods and town on fire by me, and all
The town turned out to fight for me — that held me.
I trusted the brook barrier, but feared
The road would fail; and on that side the fire
Died not without a noise of crackling wood —
Of something more than tinder grass or weed —
That brought me to my feet to hold it back

By leaning back myself, as if the reins
Were round my neck and I was at the plough.
I won! But I'm sure no one ever spread
Another color over a tenth the space
That I spread coal black over in the time
It took me. Neighbors coming home from town
Could n't believe that so much black had come there
While they had backs turned, that it had n't been there
When they had passed an hour or so before
Going the other way and they not seen it.
They looked about for someone to have done it.
But there was no one. I was somewhere wondering
Where all my weariness had gone and why
I walked so light on air in heavy shoes
In spite of a scorched Fourth of July feeling.
Why should n't I be scared remembering that?"

"If it scares you, what will it do to us?"

"Scare you. But if you shrink from being scared,
What would you say to war if it should come?
That's what for reasons I should like to know —
If you can comfort me by any answer."

"Oh, but war's not for children — it's for men."

"Now we are digging almost down to China.
My dears, my dears, you thought that — we all thought it.
So your mistake was ours. Have n't you heard, though,
About the ships where war has found them out
At sea, about the towns where war has come

Through opening clouds at night with droning speed
Further o'erhead than all but stars and angels, —
And children in the ships and in the towns?
Have n't you heard what we have lived to learn?
Nothing so new — something we had forgotten:
War is for everyone, for children too.
I was n't going to tell you, and I must n't.
The best way is to come up hill with me
And have our fire and laugh and be afraid."
   The Seven Arts   *Robert Frost*

53   *Harvest-Moon: 1914*

OVER the twilight field,
   The overflowing field, —
Over the glimmering field,
And bleeding furrows with their sodden yield
Of sheaves that still did writhe,
After the scythe;
The teeming field and darkly overstrewn
With all the garnered fulness of that noon —
Two looked upon each other.
One was a Woman men had called their mother;
And one, the Harvest-Moon.

And one, the Harvest-Moon,
Who stood, who gazed
On those unquiet gleanings where they bled;
Till the lone Woman said:

"But we were crazed . . .
We should laugh now together, I and you,
We two.
You, for your ever dreaming it was worth
A star's while to look on and light the Earth;
And I, forever telling to my mind,
Glory it was, and gladness, to give birth
To humankind!
Yes, I, that ever thought it not amiss
To give the breath to men,
For men to slay again:
Lording it over anguish but to give
My life that men might live
For this.
You will be laughing now, remembering
I called you once Dead World, and barren thing,
Yes, so we named you then,
You, far more wise
Than to give life to men."

Over the field, that there
Gave back the skies
A scattered upward stare
From blank white eyes, —
The furrowed field that lay
Striving awhile, through many a bleeding dune
Of throbbing clay, but dumb and quiet soon,
She looked; and went her way —
The Harvest-Moon.

The Boston Transcript   *Josephine Preston Peabody*

54   The Chinese Nightingale

A Song in Chinese Tapestries
Dedicated to S. T. F.

"HOW, how," he said.   "Friend Chang," I said,
"San Francisco sleeps as the dead —
Ended license, lust and play:
Why do you iron the night away?
Your big clock speaks with a deadly sound,
With a tick and a wail till dawn comes round.
While the monster shadows glower and creep,
What can be better for man than sleep?"

"I will tell you a secret," Chang replied;
"My breast with vision is satisfied,
And I see green trees and fluttering wings,
And my deathless bird from Shanghai sings."
Then he lit five fire-crackers in a pan.
"Pop, pop!" said the fire-crackers, "cra-cra-crack!"
He lit a joss-stick long and black.
Then the proud gray joss in the corner stirred;
On his wrist appeared a gray small bird:
And this was the song of the gray small bird:

"Where is the princess, loved forever,
Who made Chang first of the kings of men?"

And the joss in the corner stirred again;
And the carved dog, curled in his arms, awoke,
Barked forth a smoke-cloud that whirled and broke.

OF MAGAZINE VERSE

It piled in a maze round the ironing-place,
And there on the snowy table wide
Stood a Chinese lady of high degree,
With a scornful, witching, tea-rose face . . .
Yet she put away all form and pride,
And laid her glimmering veil aside
With a childlike smile for Chang and for me.

The walls fell back, night was aflower,
The table gleamed in a moonlit bower,
While Chang, with a countenance carved of stone,
Ironed and ironed, all alone.
And thus she sang to the busy man Chang:
"Have you forgotten . . .
Deep in the ages, long, long ago,
I was your sweetheart, there on the sand —
Storm-worn beach of the Chinese land?
We sold our grain in the peacock town
Built on the edge of the sea-sands brown —
Built on the edge of the sea-sands brown . . .

"When all the world was drinking blood
From the skulls of men and bulls,
And all the world had swords and clubs of stone,
We drank our tea in China, beneath the sacred spice-trees,
And heard the curled waves of the harbor moan.
And this gray bird, in Love's first spring,
With a bright bronze breast and a bronze-brown wing,
Captured the world with his carolling.
Do you remember, ages after,
At last the world we were born to own?
You were the heir of the yellow throne —

The world was the field of the Chinese man
And we were the pride of the sons of Han.
We copied deep books, and we carved in jade,
And wove white silks in the mulberry shade." . . .

   "I remember, I remember
That Spring came on forever,
That Spring came on forever."
Said the Chinese nightingale.

My heart was filled with marvel and dream
Though I saw the western street-lamps gleam,
Though dawn was bringing the western day,
Though Chang was a laundryman, ironing away . . .
Mingled there, with the streets and alleys,
The railroad-yard, and the clock-tower bright,
Demon-clouds crossed ancient valleys;
Across wide lotos-ponds of light
I marked a giants' firefly's flight.

And the lady, rosy-red,
Opened her fan, closed her fan,
Stretched her hand toward Chang, and said:
"Do you remember,
Ages after,
Our palace of heart-red stone?
Do you remember
The little doll-faced children
With their lanterns full of moon-fire,
That came from all the empire
Honoring the throne? —
The loveliest fête and carnival
Our world had ever known?

The sages sat about us
With their heads bowed in their beards,
With proper meditation on the sight.
Confucius was not born;
We lived in those great days
Confucius later said were lived aright . . .
And this gray bird, on that day of Spring,
With a bright-bronze breast, and a bronze-brown wing,
Captured the world with his carolling.
Late at night his tune was spent.
Peasants,
Sages,
Children,
Homeward went,
And then the bronze bird sang for you and me.
We walked alone, our hearts were high and free.
I had a silvery name, I had a silvery name,
I had a silvery name — do you remember
The name you cried beside the tumbling sea?"

   Chang turned not to the lady slim —
He bent to his work, ironing away;
But she was arch and knowing and glowing.
And the bird on his shoulder spoke for him.

   "Darling . . . darling . . . darling . . . darling . . ."
   Said the Chinese nightingale.

The great gray joss on a rustic shelf,
Rakish and shrewd, with his collar awry,
Sang impolitely, as though by himself,
Drowning with his bellowing the nightingale's cry:

"Back through a hundred, hundred years
Hear the waves as they climb the piers,
Hear the howl of the silver seas,
Hear the thunder!
Hear the gongs of holy China
How the waves and tunes combine
In a rhythmic clashing wonder,
Incantation old and fine:
   'Dragons, dragons, Chinese dragons;
    Red fire-crackers, and green fire-crackers,
    And dragons, dragons, Chinese dragons.'"

Then the lady, rosy-red,
Turned to her lover Chang and said:
"Dare you forget that turquoise dawn
When we stood on our mist-hung velvet lawn,
And worked a spell this great joss taught
Till a God of the Dragons was charmed and caught?
From the flag high over our palace-home
He flew to our feet in rainbow-foam —
A king of beauty and tempest and thunder
Panting to tear our sorrows asunder,
We mounted the back of that royal slave
With thoughts of desire that were noble and grave.

"We swam down the shore to the dragon-mountains
We whirled to the peaks and the fiery fountains.
To our secret ivory house we were borne.
We looked down the wonderful wing-filled regions
Where the dragons darted in glimmering legions.
Right by my breast the nightingale sang;

The old rhymes rang in the sunlit mist
That we this hour regain —
Song-fire for the brain.
When my hands and my hair and my feet you kissed,
When you cried for your heart's new pain,
What was my name in the dragon-mist,
In the rings of the rainbowed rain?"

   "Sorrow and love, glory and love,"
   Said the Chinese nightingale.
   "Sorrow and love, glory and love,"
   Said the Chinese nightingale.

And now the joss broke in with his song:
"Dying ember, bird of Chang,
Soul of Chang, do you remember? —
Ere you returned to the shining harbor
There were pirates by ten thousand
Descended on the town
In vessels mountain-high and red and brown,
Moon-ships that climbed the storms and cut the skies.
On their prows were painted terrible bright eyes.
But I was then a wizard and a scholar and a priest;
I stood upon the sand;
With lifted hand I looked upon them
And sunk their vessels with my wizard eyes,
And the stately lacquer-gate made safe again.
Deep, deep below the bay, the sea-weed and the spray,
Embalmed in amber every pirate lies,
Embalmed in amber every pirate lies."
Then this did the noble lady say:

"Bird, do you dream of our home-coming day
When you flew like a courier on before
From the dragon-peak to our palace-door,
And we drove the steed in your singing path —
The ramping dragon of laughter and wrath;
And found our city all aglow,
And knighted this joss that decked it so?
There were golden fishes in the purple river
And silver fishes and rainbow fishes.
There were golden junks in the laughing river,
And silver junks and rainbow junks:
There were golden lilies by the bay and river,
And silver-lilies and tiger-lilies,
And tinkling wind-bells in the gardens of the town
By the black lacquer-gate
Where walked in state
The kind king Chang
And his sweetheart mate . . .
With his flag-born dragon
And his crown of pearl . . . and . . . jade;
And his nightingale reigning in the mulberry shade,
And sailors and soldiers on the sea-sands brown,
And priests who bowed them down to your song —
By the city called Han, the peacock town,
By the city called Han, the nightingale town,
The nightingale town."
Then sang the bird, so strangely gay,
Fluttering, fluttering, ghostly and gray,
A vague, unravelling, answering tune,
Like a long unwinding silk cocoon;
Sang as though for the soul of him
Who ironed away in that bower dim:

"I have forgotten
Your dragons great,
Merry and mad and friendly and bold.
Dim is your proud lost palace-gate.
I vaguely know
There were heroes of old,
Troubles more than the heart could hold,
There were wolves in the woods
Yet lambs in the fold,
Nests in the top of the almond tree . . .
The evergreen tree . . . and the mulberry tree . . .
Life and hurry and joy forgotten
Years on years I but half-remember . . .
Man is a torch, then ashes soon,
May and June, then dead December,
Dead December, then again June.
Who shall end my dream's confusion?
Life is a loom, weaving illusion . . .
I remember, I remember
There were ghostly veils and laces . . .
In the shadowy, bowery places . . .
With lovers' ardent faces
Bending to one another,
Speaking each his part.
They infinitely echo
In the red cave of my heart.
'Sweetheart, sweetheart, sweetheart!'
They said to one another.
They spoke, I think, of perils past.
They spoke, I think, of peace at last.
One thing I remember:
Spring came on forever,

Spring came on forever,"
Said the Chinese nightingale.

Poetry: A Magazine of Verse   Vachel Lindsay

55   *He whom a Dream hath Possessed*

HE whom a dream hath possessed knoweth no more of doubting,
For a mist and the blowing of winds and the mouthing of words he scorns;
Not the sinuous speech of schools he hears, but a knightly shouting,
And never comes darkness down, yet he greeteth a million morns.

He whom a dream hath possessed knoweth no more of roaming;
All roads and the flowing of waves and the speediest flight he knows,
But wherever his feet are set, his soul is forever homing,
And going, he comes, and coming he heareth a call and goes.

He whom a dream hath possessed knoweth no more of sorrow,
At death and the dropping of leaves and the fading of suns he smiles,
For a dream remembers no past and scorns the desire of a morrow,
And a dream in a sea of doom sets surely the ultimate isles.

He whom a dream hath possessed treads the impalpable marches,
From the dust of the day's long road he leaps to a laughing star,
And the ruin of worlds that fall he views from eternal arches,
And rides God's battlefield in a flashing and golden car.
   The Forum   Shaemas O Sheel

56   *The King of Dreams*

SOME must delve when the dawn is nigh;
  Some must moil when the noonday beams;
But when the night comes, and soft winds sigh,
  Every man is a King of Dreams!

One must plod while another must ply
  At plow or loom till the sunset streams,
But when night comes, and the moon rides high,
  Every man is a King of Dreams!

One is slave to a master's cry,
  Another serf to a despot seems,
But when night comes, and the discords die,
  Every man is a King of Dreams!

This you may sell and that may buy,
  And this you may barter for gold that gleams,
But there's one domain that is fixed for aye,—
  Every man is a King of Dreams!
Lippincott's Magazine   Clinton Scollard

57 *Flammonde*

THE man Flammonde, from God knows where,
  With firm address and foreign air,
With news of nations in his talk
And something royal in his walk,
With glint of iron in his eyes,
But never doubt, nor yet surprise,
Appeared, and stayed, and held his head
As one by kings accredited.

Erect, with his alert repose
About him, and about his clothes,
He pictured all tradition hears
Of what we owe to fifty years.
His cleansing heritage of taste
Paraded neither want nor waste;
And what he needed for his fee
To live, he borrowed graciously.

He never told us what he was,
Or what mischance, or other cause,
Had banished him from better days
To play the Prince of Castaways.
Meanwhile he played surpassing well
A part, for most, unplayable;
In fine, one pauses, half afraid
To say for certain that he played.

For that, one may as well forego
Conviction as to yes or no;

Nor can I say just how intense
Would then have been the difference
To several, who, having striven
In vain to get what he was given,
Would see the stranger taken on
By friends not easy to be won.

Moreover, many a malcontent
He soothed and found munificent;
His courtesy beguiled and foiled
Suspicion that his years were soiled;
His mien distinguished any crowd,
His credit strengthened when he bowed;
And women, young and old, were fond
Of looking at the man Flammonde.

There was a woman in our town
On whom the fashion was to frown;
But while our talk renewed the tinge
Of a long-faded scarlet fringe,
The man Flammonde saw none of that,
But what he saw we wondered at —
That none of us, in her distress,
Could hide or find our littleness.

There was a boy that all agreed
Had shut within him the rare seed
Of learning. We could understand,
But none of us could lift a hand.
The man Flammonde appraised the youth,
And told a few of us the truth;
And thereby, for a little gold,
A flowered future was unrolled.

There were two citizens who fought
For years and years, and over nought;
They made life awkward for their friends,
And shortened their own dividends.
The man Flammonde said what was wrong
Should be made right; nor was it long
Before they were again in line,
And had each other in to dine.

And these I mention are but four
Of many out of many more.
So much for them. But what of him —
So firm in every look and limb?
What small satanic sort of kink
Was in his brain? What broken link
Withheld him from the destinies
That came so near to being his?

What was he, when we came to sift
His meaning, and to note the drift
Of incommunicable ways
That make us ponder while we praise?
Why was it that his charm revealed
Somehow the surface of a shield?
What was it that we never caught?
What was he, and what was he not?

How much it was of him we met
We cannot ever know; nor yet
Shall all he gave us quite atone
For what was his, and his alone;

Nor need we now, since he knew best,
Nourish an ethical unrest:
Rarely at once will nature give
The power to be Flammonde and live.

We cannot know how much we learn
From those who never will return,
Until a flash of unforeseen
Remembrance falls on what has been.
We've each a darkening hill to climb;
And this is why, from time to time
In Tilbury Town, we look beyond
Horizons for the man Flammonde.
The Outlook   *Edwin Arlington Robinson*

58   *Sandy Star*

I

SCULPTURED WORSHIP

THE zones of warmth around his heart,
   No alien airs had crossed;
But he awoke one morn to feel
   The magic numbness of autumnal frost.

His thoughts were a loose skein of threads,
   And tangled emotions, vague and dim;
And sacrificing what he loved
   He lost the dearest part of him.

In sculptured worship now he lives,
  His one desire a prisoned ache;
If he can never melt again
  His very heart will break.
The Crisis

II

LAUGHING IT OUT

He had a whim, and laughed it out
  Upon the exit of a chance;
He floundered in a sea of doubt —
  If life was real — or just romance.

Sometimes upon his brow would come
  A little pucker of defiance;
He totalled in a word the sum
  Of all man made of facts and science.

And then a hearty laugh would break,
  A reassuring shrug of shoulder;
And we would from his fancy take
  A faith in death which made life bolder.
The Crisis

III

EXIT

No, his exit by the gate
  Will not leave the wind ajar;
He will go when it is late
  With a misty star.

One will call, he cannot see;
  One will call, he will not hear;

He will take no company,
    Nor a hope or fear.

We shall smile who loved him so —
    They who gave him hate will weep;
But for us the winds will blow
    Pulsing through his sleep.

The Forum

IV

THE WAY

He could not tell the way he came,
    Because his chart was lost:
Yet all his way was paved with flame
    From the bourne he crossed.

He did not know the way to go,
    Because he had no map:
He followed where the winds blow, —
    And the April sap.

He never knew upon his brow
    The secret that he bore, —
And laughs away the mystery now
    The dark's at his door.

Scribner's Magazine

V

ONUS PROBANDI

No more from out the sunset,
    No more across the foam,
No more across the windy hills
    Will Sandy Star come home.

He went away to search it
  With a curse upon his tongue:
And in his hand the staff of life,
  Made music as it swung.

I wonder if he found it,
  And knows the mystery now —
Our Sandy Star who went away,
  With the secret on his brow.
  The Atlantic Monthly   *William Stanley Braithwaite*

59   *Saint John of Nepomuc*

LAST summer I Columbused John, in Prague, that
    deadly Bush League town —
I'd quit 'em cold on pictures and cathedrals for awhile.
I hung around for Ma and Sis (Good Lord, there was n't
    one they'd miss —
Pale martyrs till you could n't sleep, Madonnas by the
    mile!)

I read some dope in Baedeker about a tablet on the bridge,
And how they slipped this poor old scout the double cross
    for fair.
I'm off high-brow historic truck, but Father John of
    Nepomuc,
You must admit he was the goods. Believe me, he was
    there!

The king was Wenzel Number Four. John was sky-pilot
    for the court.

King gets a hunch that Mrs. King has something on her
   mind.
He goes to sleuthing more and more. He says, "Gad-
   zooks! I'll have their gore!"
(Don't ever let 'em string you on that bunk that love is
   blind!)

The queen — I'll bet she was some queen — she tangoes
   blithely on her way.
She fails to see the storm clouds on her regal husband's
   dome.
I got him guessed, that Wenzel guy harpoons a girl that's
   young and spry,
And tries to seal her up for life in the Old People's Home!

The way I had it figured out she married him to please
   her folks:
"Our son-in-law, the Kink, you know!" (Some speed!
   I guess that's poor?)
So, when she sights a Maiden's Dream — some real live
   wire that's made the team,
Well, she sits up and notices, like any girl. Why, sure!

Old Wenzel can't quite cinch the case, but what he doesn't
   know, he thinks.
The lump he calls a heart congeals beneath his fancy vest.
He sends for poor old Father John and says as follows: —
   "I am on!
I merely lack a few details! What hath the queen con-
   fessed?"

He holds the court upon the bridge. "Speak up," he
   says, " or otherwise

These spears shall thrust you down to death! Come
    through! I am the king!
Kick in! What did my spouse confess?" The queen
    sends frantic S. O. S. . . .
Maybe I sort of dozed, but well — here's how I got this
    thing . . .

He saw the startled courtiers, straining their ears;
He saw the white queen swaying, striving to stand;
He saw the soldiers tensely gripping their spears,
Waiting the king's command:
He heard a small page drawing a sobbing breath;
He heard a bird's call, poignant and sweet and low;
He heard the rush of the river, spelling death,
Mocking him, down below.
    But he only said, "My liege,
    To my honor you lay siege,
    And that fortress you can never overthrow."

He thought of how he had led them, all the years;
He thought of how he had served them, death and birth;
He thought of healing their hates, stilling their fears . . .
Humbly, he weighed his worth.
He knew he was leaving them, far from the goal;
He knew, with deep a joy, it was safe . . . and wise.
He knew that now the pale queen's pitiful soul
Would awake, and arise.
    And he only said, "My king,
    Every argument you bring
    Merely sets my duty forth in sterner guise."

He felt the spears' points, merciless, thrust him down;
He felt the exquisite, fierce glory of pain;
He felt the bright waves eager, reaching to drown,
Engulf him, body and brain.
He sensed cries, faint and clamorous, far behind;
He sensed cool peace, and the buoyant arms of love;
He sensed like a beacon, clear, beckoning, kind,
Five stars, floating above . . .
    To the ones who watched it seemed
    That he slept . . . and smiled . . . and dreamed.
    "And the waters were abated . . . and the dove."

And there I was on that old bridge — boob freshman me,
    on that same bridge!
The lazy river hummed and purred, and sang a sleepy
    song.
Of course, I know it listens queer, but, gad, it was so real
    and near,
I stood there basking in the sun for goodness knows how
    long.

Sometimes I see it even now. I see that little, lean old
    saint
Put up against the shining spears his simple nerve and
    pluck:
And once, by Jove, you know, he came right down beside
    me in the game . . .
We know who made the touchdown then, old John of
    Nepomuc!
    Poetry: A Magazine of Verse   Ruth Comfort Mitchell

60   *Samson Allen*

THERE was the drum he played so poorly,
   Though all his days he prayed for skill.
Never in life would he beat it surely,
   Even if the stars in heaven stood still.

There was the village band renewing
   Always his ancient ache to play.
It was the sum of his soul's undoing,
   And never he knew would it wear away.

Little the village found amusing,
   With no more than one straggling street,
So that without so much as choosing
   It turned to him as its jest complete.

Thus in a humor quite bucolic
   It clutched at him as its lawful prey;
Would it not add to the county's frolic
   If he should lead the band that day?

Mindful he of the vain, balked playing
   Could not take such a crown to wear;
But he would were there no gainsaying
   Beat the drum for the county fair.

With the event well worth the coming —
   All the village was there to laugh —
No matter if the clouds urged homing,
   Should not rain write his epitaph?

> Here they come with piccoli shrilling,
>   He, head high, with the raised sticks dumb —
> Now the silence that will break thrilling
>   In the crash of the rolling drum.
>
> All the years of his patient failing
>   Shrouded are by a blinding light,
> For none sees, since they all are quailing,
>   Just how the lightning made wrong right!

The Poetry Review of America   Donald Evans

61 *Gayheart*

A Story of Defeat

I

GAYHEART came in June, I saw his heels
    Go through the door, and broken heels they were.
His eyes were big, and blue, and young. He said,
    "Could you direct me to the Basement, Sir?"

I knew the Basement; I had grubbed there once
    Before a client tumbled in my net
And brought me riches. It was coffin-cold
    And on its bare walls seeped a moldy sweat.

'T was next the kitchen, too, and had the breath
    Of cheap things cooking — but I led him down.
The stairs dropped naked through the clammy dark —
    He paused, and gasped, as men do when they drown.

"Is it down there?" I turned and took his arm
  (Thin as a boy's it was; all skin and bone);
I said: "The dark is just a pleasant cloak
  To veil you off, and keep your thoughts alone.

"A Boarding-House is all-inquisitive;
  You're safer here." "How did you know," he said,
"That I would want to be alone? Am I
  An open book to be so simply read?"

We stumbled down until I felt the door
  Beneath my fingers. Then I struck a light —
The room grinned at us like an ugly face
  Caught in a heart-beat from the cloak of night.

The boy's breath cracked his lips. I saw his soul
  Stand in his eyes, and look, and shrink again,
Sick with the moment's shattered visionings,
  And on his face went the slow feet of pain.

"It strikes you bleak, eh? Come, it's not so bad.
  The gas won't whimper if you turn it low.
The bed is lame, but friendly. Here's a desk
  To scribble at." He said: "I write, you know.

"I've come to be a writer." And he smiled,
  As boys do when they say their heart's desire;
"I'm from the South — a paper took me on,
  But that's just keeping fagots in my fire."

He smiled again, for he had all his youth
  To smile from. "My real work," he said, "will be
To sketch the city — not in prosy books,
  But in its native, living poetry.

"Cities were made for measures and for rhyme,
　They have an ancient minstrelsy of feet,
And rivers sweep their shipping like a song,
　And there is endless music in a street.

"Endless, I say, and never caught by man.
　Your books?　Ah, how they walk, walk, walk, with words;
But verse runs on light feet, as Cities do —
　O God, I've dreamed it till it hurts like swords

"Not to be writing; but I've got to learn,
　Learn, learn it all — the streets, the parks, the ships,
The subway and the skyscrapers!"　He stopped
　And brushed his hand across his trembling lips.

"Excuse me, sir.　You were the first kind soul
　I'd spoken to — the rest are like the tomb."
He smiled and touched my hand; and then I turned,
　Leaving him standing in his wistful room.

II

June passed, and weather came that seared our flesh.
　The soft streets crawled; old men dropped down and died;
Within the House our summer tempers snarled,
　And every night the lady boarder cried.

Her alcove shouldered mine — and so I knew.
　She came at six, her feet as slow as lead
Dragged through her door, and cried till supper-time.
　I never saw her but her eyes were red.

Poor Gayheart whitened slowly, till his face
  Was like the paper that he scribbled on.
But he had youth, and some vague bravery
  That held him taut until his task was done.

He rasped our nerves, though, with his restless ways,
  His restless, silent ways. . . . He never seemed
To see us when we passed him in the hall —
  His eyes were distant with the thing he dreamed.

He bolted dinner like a dog, as though
  He feared his fate would snatch him unaware
With all his dreams unproved — then, starting up,
  Would grope the shadowed hallway to the stair,

And down to his eternal folderol,
  His spitting gaslight and his scratching pen,
Until we cursed him for his industry,
  His being different from the ruck of men.

Then one dead night when all the stars did sweat
  He plucked my sleeve, and smiled, and drew me down
His damned black stairs. Then, while the clogged jet whined,
  He read me what he'd written of the Town.

It struck me wonderful. It had the ache
  Of rush-hour traffic in it, and the swing
Of wheels, as though he'd listened in a street,
  A crowded street where life ran thundering. . . .

It made me think of going to my work;
  Of men in crowds, and women's faces drawn
With painted lines, and shops and ships and spires
  And skyscrapers that reached up for the dawn.

And then beneath the step of rhyme I heard
   The boy's soul speaking. . . . And I knew that he
Had spent himself like dust among the crowd
   To catch the heart-beat for his poetry.

His voice went out like flame.. I found myself
   Shocked by the still, small room. To me it seemed
Great throngs had passed with various noise. He said:
   "That's just the gateway to the thing I've dreamed!"

III

There is a street's end, where the coasters sleep,
   And there, at twilight, purple waters run,
And o'er their breast the crimson-coated day
   Trails the last silver of the fallen sun.

A wall is there, for men to dream upon;
   And so young Gayheart went, with all his scars
Unhealed . . . and saw the lights sown through the dusk,
   And his tall city in a cloak of stars.

Tier upon tier the golden windows burned,
   As though men sought new freedom in the skies;
And somehow, lured by starlight and by dawn,
   Built his blind cities up to paradise!

Afar the bridges spun their silver webs,
   The mellow whistles talked along the stream;
But Gayheart leaned athirst upon a stone,
   Hurt with the shining beauty of his dream.

And he was like a child with wistfulness,
   Holding his hands out through the summer night,
Where in the dusk the great, clean towers flared,
   Like swords thrust up in some red battle-light!

And then he turned, all dumb with his desire,
   And stumbled through still streets, until he found
The great bridge trembling underfoot and heard
   The trains go by him with a tempest sound.

Black, shapeless forms came shrieking with bright eyes;
   The sea-wind rolled like drums against his ears,
And he was singing, singing as he trod,
   And in his eyes were sudden, smarting tears.

The tallest spire enraptured him! He strode
   Under the roofed bridge, where the newsboys cry,
And out into that little breathing-space
   From whence the windows go into the sky.

And there he sought a bench and sat him down,
   Between two snoring vagabonds, who lay
Sprawled on their faces, . . . but his wakefulness
   Was like a lamp within him till the day.

   . . . .

What did it mean? the stone flung like a song?
   The desk-light brothering the star? The whole
Up-sweep of roofs that is our native-land —
   What meaning had it, and what secret soul?

He sat with upturned eyes, as young men do,
   Until the lamp upon his face grew wan;
He saw his nation toiling in its House,
   Its tall, strange House that reached up for the dawn!

And dreaming, saw the Elder Worlds asleep
   In their low houses, beautiful with Time. . . .
The vagrant at his left side groaned and breathed,
   Lifting a face of cumulative grime —

"What's in yer gizzard, lad, that twists ye so?
   I know! You're one of them wot's got a brain!
Now me —" His brother raised a blowzy head:
   "Aw, hell!" he snarled, and fell asleep again.

Across the roofs the first, faint gold of dawn
   Streaked the dun heavens, and the Day Men took
The windows of the sleepless, so that life
   Went smoothly like a never-written book.

And Gayheart shook the cramps from his dull limbs,
   Rose and went up the paper's curling stair
Until he reached the City Room. The Staff,
   Half stripped of cloth, already sweated there.

But he dropped at his crazy, limping desk,
   In the dim corner where the cubs are kept,
And wrote: "*America is wakefulness!*"
   And fell face upon the words, and slept.

IV

Gayheart's book came back, and back again,
   And still he mailed it out, with little lies
To cloak its failure — but I think we saw
   The naked, frightened soul behind his eyes.

The lady boarder knew. I heard her say
    A cruel thing: "Your book is home," she said,
"For Sunday dinner." But he passed her by
    Without the slightest turning of his head.

She hated him. . . . And so mid-autumn fell,
    With no abating coolness. Each new sun
Was like a murderer let out of locks,
    And life went sickly, praying to be done.

A night fell when all sleep was vain. . . . I rose
    And stumbled to the windowful of stars,
That was my share of heaven. . . . There I stood
    Letting the soft night seep into my scars.

The window opened on a little court,
    And suddenly a feeble thrust of flame
Stabbed like a pettish dagger through the dark,
    Out of the night a ragged breathing came.

. . . I saw the Basement boarder stooping down,
    His lean face bloodied with the touch of light.
A tongue of fire licked his hands . . . and died,
    Brief as the flutter of a star in flight.

Somehow I sensed a tragedy. . . . The gloom
    Was like a grave, the light leaped up no more.
I turned and groped down through the breathless house;
    Until I saw him crouching by his door.

He stood there, staring at his empty hands
    As though they'd done his dearest dream to death;
The palms were soiled and smeared with paper ash;
    There was a reek of whisky on his breath.

"What's this?" I said. He raised his head and smiled
  With a deep drunkenness that touched his soul.
"I'll tell you what it is! I've been a fool —
  The sort of fool that makes a dream his goal.

"I've worked my heart out; done a decent thing —
  And no one wants it! No one wants to look
Beneath the surface of this world of ours.
  It's all damned artifice. . . . I've burned my book."

Even to me the thing seemed tragical —
  As though he'd set a torch to half himself.
"What!" I cried, "burned your splendid poetry?
  Laid yourself out like that upon a shelf?

"What will you do?" "I'll do as other men;
  Harness my talent as a modern should.
I'll do the obvious with all my age —
  The cheap, the counterfeit, the understood!

"I've a new job this night; a fine, new job —"
  He spat into the shadows of the place —
"Verse-making on a magazine! The sort
  That wears a painted simper on its face.

"I'm rich . . . and drunk. I had to drink or scream,
  And drink goes deep with me; . . . get me to bed.
I've slaughter on my soul — and verse to make.
  My editor wants — something light — he said —

"Something that's brisk and — funny!" There he stood,
  With those raw, suffering eyes and stared at me,
Until I near cried out. He was so white!
  And older . . . older than a man should be.

I swear whole ages crumbled in his face,
   For he had dreamed, and dreams are ancient things,
Bearing a harsher reckoning than Time
   When once despair has crumbled up their wings.

I got him stripped and into bed at last,
   The poor, spent lad! He lay there still and stark,
His smudged hands clenched across his shallow chest,
   And moaned once as I crept out through the dark.

    . . . .

Success came to him swiftly; made him drunk.
   He gulped life as a drunkard gulps his bowl,
Forgetting all his splendid futile dreams —
   He was an altered person to his soul.

He fattened and grew flushed; he learned to sneer;
   His verses ran like swift, malignant flame,
Smirching the thing they touched and burning on
   To wipe the pathway for his striding fame.

He left the Basement then; soared up two flights
   With braggart wings, bought furniture and prints,
Nonsense, we called it! — and to crown the show
   Decked out his trappings in a flowered chintz.

But that phase passed. His true self's tide flowed back,
   We saw him drowning in his own strange deeps;
A crawling restlessness crept from his eyes,
   The sort of serpent thing that never sleeps.

A month or two he clung to his gay nest,
   Beat his wings breathlessly within a shell,
Made himself live with all his flaunted things,
   Grim as a tortured convict in a cell.

And then his self's self conquered. . . . One May night
   When earth was breathing fragrance to its core,
And open windows drank the breath of Spring,
   He came and stood within my open door.

"Please," he said, "would you mind?" . . . And there
   he stopped,
   Sucking his cheeks in like a timid boy.
"I've gone back to the Basement. . . . I've gone back!
   The other room made life seem just a toy.

"And that's not right. . . . There's something more to
   life
   Than turning it to playthings. . . . I've gone back,
To find my book again, to do the work
   I'd planned to do according to my knack."

"Your book," I said, "your book? You burned it, boy!"
   He flinched. "I know. I feel its ashes still
Here on my hands. That's what I want of you —
   I know that you can help me if you will."

His tone was light, and yet I heard him breathe
   As men do in the ache and grip of strife.
I rose and went with him. Again he said,
   "There's something more than toys to make of life."

The Basement, with its yellow tooth of light,
   Grinned at us like a long-familiar face,
Whose daily wont of ugliness, revealed,
   Mounts to a sin within the moment's space.

Its gaping door still breathed the winter's chill,
   Its single window level with the street
Flickered with fragments of the passing world,
   Hummed with a whispered drudgery of feet.

And yet to him its very barrenness
   Was like a savage penance. Standing there
He bruised himself upon its ugliness
   Until the sweat stood out beneath his hair.

"I asked you down," he said, "to help me think,
   To help remember." Once again the sweat
Stood out on him, and as I looked I knew
   It was his soul had made his body wet.

He gripped me with the hunger of his eyes,
   Hard as a knife his glance was, hard as steel.
"How did it go? — My book? I've thought and thought
   Until my brain is like a going wheel."

I stared at him in sudden choking pain.
   "Boy!" I said. "For my life —" He cried, "You
     must!
It's all behind a door inside your mind;
   It's there, if you will brush aside the dust!

"My own mind's locked against me. Now and then
   A line comes back, a bare crumb at the most.
My plan, my meaning — all the soul within
   Peers with faded features of a ghost."

"It was the Town," I said, "in all its guise.
   The Town! It was the crowds along the street;
Faces and spires and stately ships and dreams,
   Desires, and winnings, and I think — defeat."

"Defeat," he gasped, "defeat!" And then he dropped
   Down at his palsied desk and bowed his head
Upon his arms. . . . I felt my flesh grow cold
   As though that gesture meant a man struck dead.

"Oh," he said, from the prison of his arms,
   "What god would wreck a man with one mistake?
Give him two selves and to each self a sword
   So he's half slain or ever he's awake!"

He raised his haggard face. "In every man
   There is division of the dust and dream,
And Youth is just the crossing of the swords
   Before he takes his place within the scheme.

"The Town's a citadel for all things flesh,
   And yet a man might storm it with a song,
Played he not traitor to himself . . . I quit,
   And oh, it was the quitting that was wrong!

"I was so lonely for a thing to love,
   A single look, a passing word of praise —
I was as near to triumph as a smile,
   And now defeat, defeat for all my days!

"Cities are cruel things," he whispered then,
   "Their slaves are Failure, and their gods Defeat."
In at the window came a thrust of wind,
   Bearing the weary music of the street . . .

He leaped up with an oath, snapped off the light,
   An instant, unforgetable, there gleamed
His white face. . . . Then a whisper through the dark,
   "I would to God that I had never dreamed."

   . . . .

The years go slowly in a boarding-house,
　　Sharpened with neither passions nor despairs;
Time seems to falter in those dim, gray halls —
　　The days are only footsteps on the stairs.

The Basement yawned for tenants, but none came;
　　It seemed completer for its emptiness.
Gayheart had been its last . . . To me the room
　　Still wore the mantle of his soul's distress.

I never saw his face but once again;
　　It was a sharp cold midnight in the fall;
Broadway lay flaming like a polished sword,
　　As though one night were given to flame its all.

The theaters, bright-mouthed, poured forth a stream
　　Of pallid faces that the glare struck dead.
The street crawled, and the noise went up to God
　　In formless cries, like some great need unsaid.

The buffet of false brightness swept the night
　　With rosy blushes to the firmament.
Here ran the riot of a hoarded world,
　　Here life was only reckoned to be spent!

And here, carved in that graceless art of fire,
　　Stood Gayheart's name, a star's height o'er the street.
His words came back to me as clear as bells,
　　"*Their slaves are Failure, and their gods Defeat!*"

Was this defeat, then? Was his fame defeat?
　　I knew the sort of comic thing he'd done.
Had he forgot those ashes on his hands?
　　Had he by hard forgetting played and won?

Then suddenly I saw him in the crowd,
  Beneath that scarlet flaunting of his name.
A smooth, smug mask of flesh was on him now;
  He was the very creature of his fame.

His boyishness had died. . . . His hard, clean youth
  Was gone forever 'neath a whelm of clay.
Yet as I looked I saw him lift his head,
  And all his grossness seemed to fall away.

His hungry look went straight to Heaven's throne,
  High up into the folded book of stars,
And on his face I saw the Quest again —
  He was the seeker, fainting with his scars!

One glimpse and he was gone, . . . a soul blown on
  And lost at last beneath those painted skies.
Yet he still lives! There never dawns a day
  But I behold him in the City's eyes.
The North American Review   Dana Burnet

62   *The Unconquered Air*

I

OTHERS endure Man's rule: he therefore deems
  I shall endure it — I, the unconquered Air!
    Imagines this triumphant strength may bear
His paltry sway! yea, ignorantly dreams,
Because proud Rhea now his vassal seems,
  And Neptune him obeys in billowy lair,
  That he a more sublime assault may dare,
Where blown by tempest wild the vulture screams!

Presumptuous, he mounts: I toss his bones
    Back from the height supernal he has braved:
Ay, as his vessel nears my perilous zones,
I blow the cockle-shell away like chaff,
    And give him to the Sea he has enslaved.
He founders in its depths; and then I laugh!

II

Impregnable I held myself, secure
    Against intrusion. Who can measure Man?
    How should I guess his mortal will outran
Defeat so far that danger could allure
For its own sake? — that he would all endure,
    All sacrifice, all suffer, rather than
    Forego the daring dreams Olympian
That prophesy to him of victory sure?

Ah, tameless courage! — dominating power
That, all attempting, in a deathless hour
    Made earth-born Titans godlike, in revolt! —
Fear is the fire that melts Icarian wings:
Who fears nor Fate, nor Time, nor what Time brings,
    May drive Apollo's steeds, or wield the thunderbolt!

Harper's Magazine   *Florence Earle Coates*

63   *A Likeness*

Portrait Bust of an Unknown, Capitol, Rome

IN every line a supple beauty —
    The restless head a little bent —
Disgust of pleasure, scorn of duty,
    The unseeing eyes of discontent.

OF MAGAZINE VERSE

I often come to sit beside him,
   This youth who passed and left no trace
Of good or ill that did betide him,
   Save the disdain upon his face.

The hope of all his House, the brother
   Adored, the golden-hearted son,
Whom Fortune pampered like a mother;
   And then — a shadow on the sun.
Whether he followed Cæsar's trumpet,
   Or chanced the riskier game at home
To find how favor played the strumpet
   In fickle politics at Rome;

Whether he dreamed a dream in Asia
   He never could forget by day,
Or gave his youth to some Aspasia,
   Or gamed his heritage away;
Once lost, across the Empire's border
   This man would seek his peace in vain;
His look arraigns a social order
   Somehow entrammelled with his pain.

"The dice of gods are always loaded";
   One gambler, arrogant as they,
Fierce, and by fierce injustice goaded,
   Left both his hazard and the play.
Incapable of compromises,
   Unable to forgive or spare,
The strange awarding of the prizes
   He had no fortitude to bear.

Tricked by the forms of things material —
   The solid-seeming arch and stone,
The noise of war, the pomp imperial,
   The heights and depths about a throne —
He missed, among the shapes diurnal,
   The old, deep-travelled road from pain,
The thoughts of men which are eternal,
   In which, eternal, men remain.

Ritratto d'ignoto; defying
   Things unsubstantial as a dream —
An Empire, long in ashes lying —
   His face still set against the stream.
Yes, so he looked, that gifted brother
   I loved, who passed and left no trace,
Not even — luckier than this other —
   His sorrow in a marble face.

Scribner's Magazine   *Willa Sibert Cather*

64   *On a Copy of Keats' "Endymion"*

HAS not the glamoured season come once more,
   When earth puts on her arras of soft green?
See where along the meadow rillet's shore
   The wild-rose buds unfold!
     Eastward the boughs with murmurous laughter lean
     To warm themselves in morning's generous gold.
The foxgloves nod along the English lanes
   That saw erewhile the dancing sprites of snow;
Night-long the leaf-hid nightingale complains
   With such melodious woe

That Sleep, enamored of her soaring strains,
   Is widely wakeful as the dim hours go.

Ope but the page — and hark, the impassioned bird
   That through the hush of the be-shadowed hours
Pours in the ear of dark its melting word!
      Here is as mellow song
   As ever welled from pleachèd laurel bowers,
      Or e'er was borne soft orient winds along;
Here may one list all ecstasies they sung,
   The shepherds and the maids of Arcady,
   Flower-garlanded what time the world was young; —
   Pandean minstrelsy,
Low flutings from slim pipes of silver tongue
   Played by the dryads on some upland lea.

And blent with these are heavenly whisperings
   As faint as whitening poplars make at dawn,
   Sublime suggestions of fine-fingered strings
      Touched in celestial air,
   And earthward through the dulling ether drawn,
      Yet falling on us more than earthly fair;
The voice divine that young Endymion knew
   In the cool woodland's darkmost depths by night,
When godlike ardors thrilled him through and through;
      And his voice from the height
Whither, on wakening, drenched with chilly dew,
   He sought the goddess in the gathering light.

But ah, what mournful memories are mine,
   Song-wakened at this lavish summer-tide!
Can I forget that sombre cypress line

    By old Rome's ruined wall,
  The lonely grave that alien grasses hide,
    And the pathetic silence shrouding all?
Who would forget? Blest be the song that bears
    My soul across aerial seas of space
As wingèdly as airy fancy fares!
    For now that earth's worn face
The radiant glow of life's renewal wears,
    Would I in reverence seek that sacred place.

There would I lay these woven shreds of rhyme
    In lieu of scattered heart's-ease and the rose.
Behold how Song has triumphed over Time,
    For still *his* song rings clear,
      Though where the tender Roman violet grows
    Deep has he slumbered many a fateful year!
If to the poet's rapt imaginings
    Beauty be wed, with love of purpose high,
Despite the cynic and his scornful flings
    Song shall not fail and die,
But like the bird that up the azure springs
    Still thrill the heart, still fill the listening sky!
The North American Review   Clinton Scollard

65   *Silence*

I HAVE known the silence of the stars and of the sea,
  And the silence of the city when it pauses,
And the silence of a man and a maid,
And the silence for which music alone finds the word,

And the silence of the woods before the winds of spring
    begin,
And the silence of the sick
When their eyes roam about the room.
And I ask: For the depths
Of what use is language?
A beast of the fields moans a few times
When death takes its young.
And we are voiceless in the presence of realities —
We cannot speak.

   A curious boy asks an old soldier
Sitting in front of the grocery store,
"How did you lose your leg?"
And the old soldier is struck with silence,
Or his mind flies away
Because he cannot concentrate it on Gettysburg.
It comes back jocosely
And he says, "A bear bit it off."
And the boy wonders, while the old soldier
Dumbly, feebly lives over
The flashes of guns, the thunder of cannon,
The shrieks of the slain,
And himself lying on the ground,
And the hospital surgeons, the knives,
And the long days in bed.
But if he could describe it all
He would be an artist.
But if he were an artist there would be deeper wounds
Which he could not describe.

   There is the silence of a great hatred,
And the silence of a great love,

And the silence of a deep peace of mind,
And the silence of an embittered friendship,
There is the silence of a spiritual crisis,
Through which your soul, exquisitely tortured,
Comes with visions not to be uttered
Into a realm of higher life.
And the silence of the gods who understand each other
 without speech,
There is the silence of defeat.
There is the silence of those unjustly punished;
And the silence of the dying whose hand
Suddenly grips yours.
There is the silence between father and son,
When the father cannot explain his life,
Even though he be misunderstood for it.

   There is the silence that comes between husband and
 wife.
There is the silence of those who have failed;
And the vast silence that covers
Broken nations and vanquished leaders.
There is the silence of Lincoln,
Thinking of the poverty of his youth.
And the silence of Napoleon
After Waterloo.
And the silence of Jeanne d'Arc
Saying amid the flames, "Blessed Jesus" —
Revealing in two words all sorrow, all hope.
And there is the silence of age,
Too full of wisdom for the tongue to utter it
In words intelligible to those who have not lived
The great range of life.

And there is the silence of the dead.
If we who are in life cannot speak
Of profound experiences,
Why do you marvel that the dead
Do not tell you of death?
Their silence shall be interpreted
As we approach them.
Poetry: A Magazine of Verse   Edgar Lee Masters

66   *Miracles*

I

TWILIGHT is spacious, near things in it seem far,
  And distant things seem near.
Now in the green west hangs a yellow star.
And now across old waters you may hear
The profound gloom of bells among still trees,
Like a rolling of huge boulders beneath seas.

Silent as though in evening contemplation
Weaves the bat under the gathering stars.
Silent as dew we seek new incarnation,
Meditate new avatars.
In a clear dusk like this
Mary climbed up the hill to seek her son,
To lower him down from the cross, and kiss
The mauve wounds, every one.

Men with wings
In the dusk walked softly after her.
She did not see them, but may have felt
The winnowed air around her stir.

She did not see them, but may have known
Why her son's body was light as a little stone.
She may have guessed that other hands were there
Moving the watchful air.

Now, unless persuaded by searching music
Which suddenly opens the portals of the mind,
We guess no angels,
And are content to be blind.
Let us blow silver horns in the twilight.
And lift our hearts to the yellow star in the green,
To find, perhaps, if while the dew is rising,
Clear things may not be seen.

II

Under a tree I sit, and cross my knees,
And smoke a cigarette.
You nod to me: you think perhaps you know me.
But I escape you, I am none of these;
I leave my name behind me, I forget . . .

I hear a fountain shattering into a pool;
I see the gold fish slanting under the cool;
And suddenly all is frozen into silence.
And among the firs, or over desert grass,
Or out of a cloud of dust, or out of darkness,
Or on the first slow patter of sultry rain,
I hear a voice cry "Marvels have come to pass, —
The like of which shall not be seen again!"

And behold, across a sea one came to us,
Treading the wave's edge with his naked feet,
Slowly, as one might walk in a ploughed field.

We stood where the soft waves on the shingle beat,
In a blowing mist, and pressed together in terror,
And marvelled that all our eyes might share one error.

For if the fishes' fine-spun net must sink,
Or pebbles flung by a boy, or the thin sand,
How shall we understand
That flesh and blood might tread on the sea water
And foam not wet the ankles?   We must think
That all we know is lost, or only a dream,
That dreams are real, and real things only dream.

And if a man may walk to us like this
On the unstable sea, as on a beach,
With his head bowed in thought —
Then we have been deceived in what men teach;
And all our knowledge has come to nought;
And a little flame should seek the earth,
And leaves, falling, should seek the sky,
And surely we should enter the womb for birth,
And sing from the ashes when we die.

Or was the man a god, perhaps, or devil?
They say he healed the sick by stroke of hands;
And that he gave the sights of the earth to the blind.
And I have heard that he could touch a fig-tree,
And say to it, "Be withered!" and it would shrink
Like a cursed thing, and writhe its leaves, and die.
How shall we understand such things, I wonder,
Unless there are things invisible to the eye?

And there was Lazarus, raised from the dead:
To whom he spoke, quietly, in the dusk, —
Lazarus, three days dead, and mortified;

And the pale body trembled; as from a swoon,
Sweating, the sleeper woke, and raised his head;
And turned his puzzled eyes from side to side . . .

Should we not, then, hear voices in a stone,
Whispering softly of heaven and hell?
Or if one walked beside a sea, alone,
Hear broodings of a bell? . . .
Or on a green hill in the evening's fire,
If we should stand and listen to poplar trees,
Should we not hear the lit leaves suddenly choir
A jargon of silver music against the sky? . . .
Or the dew sing, or dust profoundly cry? . . .
If this is possible, then all things are:
And I may leave my body crumpled there
Like an old garment on the floor;
To walk abroad on the unbetraying air;
To pass through every door,
And see the hills of the earth, or climb a stair.

Wound me with spears, you only stab the wind;
You nail my cloak against a bitter tree;
You do not injure me.

I pass through the crowd, the dark crowd busy with
    murder,
Through the linked arms I pass;
And slowly descend the hill through dew-wet grass.

III

Twilight is spacious, near things in it seem far,
And distant things seem near.
Now in the green west hangs a yellow star;
And now across old waters you may hear

The profound gloom of bells among still trees,
Like a rolling of huge boulders beneath seas.

Peter said that Christ, though crucified,
Had not died;
But that escaping from his cerements,
In human flesh, with mortal sense,
Amazed at such an ending,
He fled alone, and hid in Galilee,
And lived in secret, spending
His days and nights, perplexed, in contemplation:
And did not know if this were surely he.

Did Peter tell me this?   Or was I Peter?
Or did I listen to a tavern-story?
Green leaves thrust out and fall.   It was long ago.
Dust has been heaped upon us. . . . We have perished.
We clamor again.   And again we are dust and blow.

Well, let us take the music, and drift with it
Into the darkness. . . . It is exquisite.
The Poetry Journal   Conrad Aiken

67   *Ash Wednesday*

(After hearing a lecture on the origins of religion)

HERE in the lonely chapel I will wait,
   Here will I rest, if any rest may be;
So fair the day is, and the hour so late,
I shall have few to share the blessed calm with me.
Calm and soft light, sweet inarticulate calls!

One shallow dish of eerie golden fire
By molten chains above the altar swinging,
Draws my eyes up from the shadowed stalls
To the warm chancel-dome;
Crag-like the clustered organs loom,
Yet from their thunder-threatening choir
Flows but a ghostly singing —
Half-human voices reaching home
In infinite, tremulous surge and falls.
Light on his stops and keys,
And pallor on the player's face,
Who, listening rapt, with finger-skill to seize
The pattern of a mood's elusive grace,
Captures his spirit in an airy lace
Of fading, fading harmonies.
Oh, let your coolness soothe
My weariness, frail music, where you keep
Tryst with the even-fall;
Where tone by tone you find a pathway smooth
To yonder gleaming cross, or nearer creep
Along the bronzèd wall,
Where shade by shade thro' deeps of brown
Comes the still twilight down.

Wilt thou not rest, my thought?
Wouldst thou go back to that pain-breeding room
Whence only by strong wrenchings thou wert brought?
O weary, weary questionings,
Will ye pursue me to the altar rail
Where my old faith for sanctuary clings,
And back again my heart reluctant hale
Yonder, where crushed against the cheerless wall

OF MAGAZINE VERSE

Tiptoe I glimpsed the tier on tier
Of faces unserene and startled eyes —
Such eyes as on grim surgeon-work are set,
On desperate outmaneuverings of doom?
Still must I hear
The boding voice with cautious rise and fall
Tracking relentless to its lair
Each fever-bred progenitor of faith,
Each fugitive ancestral fear?
Still must I follow, as the wraith
Of antique awe toward a wreck-making beach
Drives derelict?
Nay, rest, rest, my thought,
Where long-loved sound and shadow teach
Quietness to conscience overwrought.

Harken! The choristers, the white-robed priest
Move thro' the chapel dim
Sounding of warfare and the victor's palm,
Of valiant marchings, of the feast
Spread for the pilgrim in a haven'd calm.
How on the first lips of my steadfast race
Sounded that battle hymn,
Quaint heaven-vauntings, with God's gauntlet flung,
To me bequeathed, from age to age,
My challenge and my heritage!
"The Lord is in His holy place" —
How in their ears the herald voice has rung!
Now will I make bright their sword,
Will pilgrim in their ancient path,
Will haunt the temple of their Lord;
Truth that is neither variable nor hath

Shadow of turning, I will find
In the wise ploddings of their faithful mind:
Of finding not, as in this frustrate hour
By question hounded, waylaid by despair,
Yet in these uses shall I know His power
As the warm flesh by breathing knows the air.

O futile comfort! My faith-hungry heart
Still in your sweetness tastes a poisonous sour;
Far off, far off I quiver 'neath the smart
Of old indignities and obscure scorn
Indelibly on man's proud spirit laid,
That now in time's ironic masquerade
Minister healing to the hurt and worn!
What are those streams that from the altar pour
Where goat and ox and human captive bled
To feed the blood-lust of the murderous priest?
I cannot see where Christ's dear love is shed,
So deep the insatiate horror washes red
Flesh-stains and frenzy-sears and gore.
Beneath that Cross, whereon His hands outspread,
What forest shades behold what shameful rites
Of maidenhood surrendered to the beast
In obscene worship on midsummer nights!
What imperturbable disguise
Enwraps these organs with a chaste restraint
To chant innocuous hymns and litanies
For sinner and adoring saint,
Which yet inherit like an old blood-taint
Some naked caperings in the godliest tune, —
Goat-songs and jests strong with the breath of Pan,
That charmed the easy cow-girl and her man

In uncouth tryst beneath a scandalous moon!
Ah, could I harken with their trust,
Or see with their pure-seeing eyes
Who of the frame of these dear mysteries
Were not too wise!
Why cannot I, as in a stronger hour,
Outface the horror that defeats me now?
Have I not reaped complacent the rich power
That harvest from this praise and bowing low?
On this strong music have I mounted up,
At yonder rail broke bread, and shared the holy cup,
And on that cross have hung, and felt God's pain
Sorrowing, sorrowing, till the world shall end.

Not from these forms my questionings come
That serving truth are purified,
But from the truth itself, the way, the goal,
One challenge vast that strikes faith dumb —
If truth be fickle, who shall be our guide?
"Truth that is neither variable, nor hath
Shadow of turning?"   Ah, where turns she not!
Where yesterday she stood,
Now the horizon empties — lo, her steps
Where yonder scholar woos, are hardly cold,
Yet shall he find her never, but the thought
Mantling within him like her blood
Shall from his eloquence fade, and leave his words
Flavor'd with vacant quaintness for his son.
What crafty patience, scholar, hast thou used,
Useless ere it was begun —
What headless waste of wing,
Beating vainly round and round!

In no one Babel were the tongues confused,
But they who handle truth, from sound to sound
Master another speech continuously.
Deaf to familiar words, our callous ear
Will quiver to the edge of utterance strange;
When truth to God's truth-weary sight draws near,
Cannot God see her till she suffer change?
Must ye then change, my vanished youth,
Home customs of my dreams?
Change and farewell!
Farewell, your lost phantasmic truth
That will not constant dwell,
But flees the passion of our eyes
And leaves no hint behind her
Whence she dawns or whither dies,
Or if she live at all, or only for a moment seems.

Here tho' I only dream I find her,
Here will I watch the twilight darken.
Yonder the scholar's voice spins on
Mesh upon mesh of loveless fate;
Here will I rest while truth deserts him still.
What hath she left thee, Brother, but thy voice?
After her, have thy will,
And happy be thy choice!
Here rather will I rest, and harken
Voices longer dead but longer loved than thine.

Yet still my most of peace is more unrest,
As one who plods a summer road
Feels the coolness his own motion stirs,
But when he stops the dead heat smothers him.
Here in this calm my soul is weariest,

Each question with malicious goad
Pressing the choice that still my soul defers
To visioned hours not thus eclipsed and dim,
Lest in my haste I deem
That truth's invariable part
Is her eluding of man's heart.
Farewell, calm priest who pacest slow
After the stalwart-marching choir!
Have men thro' thee taught God their dear desire?
Hath God thro' thee absolvèd sin?
What is thy benediction, if I go
Sore perplexed and wrought within?
Open the chapel doors, and let
Boisterous music play us out
Toward the flaring molten west
Whither the nerve-racked day is set;
Let the loud world, flooding back,
Gulf us in its hungry rout;
Rest? What part have we in rest?

Boy with the happy face and hurrying feet,
Who with thy friendly cap's salute
Sendest bright hail across the college street,
If thou couldst see my answering lips, how mute,
How loth to take thy student courtesy!
What truth have I for thee?
Rather thy wisdom, lad, impart,
Share thy gift of strength with me.
Still with the past I wrestle, but the future girds thy heart.
Clutter of shriveled yesterdays that clothe us like a shell,
Thy spirit sloughs their bondage off, to walk newborn and
    free.

All things the human heart hath learned — God, heaven,
    earth, and hell —
Thou weighest not for what they were, but what they
    still may be.
Whether the scholar delve and mine for faith-wreck
    buried deep,
Or the priest his rules and holy rites, letter and spirit,
    keep,
Toil or trust in breathless dust, they shall starve at last
    for truth;
Scholar and priest shall live from thee, who art eternal
    youth.
Holier if thou dost tread it, every path the prophets trod;
Clearer where thou dost worship, rise the ancient hymns
    to God;
Not by the priest but by thy prayers are altars sanctified;
Strong with new love where thou dost kneel, the cross
    whereon Christ died.

The Yale Review   *John Erskine*

68   *To a Logician*

COLD man, in whom no animating ray
    Warms the chill substance of the sculptor's clay;
Grim Reasoner, with problems in your eyes,
Professor, Sage — however do they call you?
Far-seeing Blindman, fame shall yet befall you;
Carve you in stone — that Winter of the wise! —
And set you up in some pale portico
To frown on heaven above, on earth below.

I shall make songs, and give them to the breeze,
And die amid a thousand ecstasies!
I shall be dust, and feel the joyous sting
Of that sweet arrow from the bow of Time
Which men call Spring.
And out of my dead mouth a rose shall come like rhyme!
But you, in your eternal state of snows,
Shall thrill no more to life's resurgent flood,
Nor cast death's laughter into April's rose!
You shall be marble, who were never blood.
  Harper's Magazine   Dana Burnet

69   *The Clerk*

"TWO and two are four, four and three are seven"—
    That is all that he can say where he sits in Heaven;
"Two and two are four, four and three are seven"—
Through the long celestial day.

"Two and two are four, four and three are seven"—
Once he used to sing it down the halls of Heaven;
"Work is hard but there's an answer,
Far ahead great things are waiting,
I will add the magic Figures,
I will seek the gleaming Balance—
I will win the Master's praise."

"Two and two are four, four and three are seven"—
Not so careful now in the place of Heaven;
"Work is good but there is pleasure,
I am young with time before me—
O bright angel, from the shops of Heaven,

Dance awhile, the Harper's playing —
Drink the rainbow wine with me!"

"Two and two are four, four and three are seven"
Then he only droned it on his stool in Heaven;
"Work is bread and bread is living,
Little mouths grow very hungry
In the rooms of Paradise —
She must wear a golden feather
When she walks along the sky."

"Two and two are four, four and three are seven" —
Just a whisper now through the walls of Heaven;
"O I can not find the error,
Can not strike the gleaming Balance —
All the magic's out of Figures,
All the wonder out of loving,
And the Master has no praise."

"Two and two are four, four and three are seven" —
Still he mutters on at the books of Heaven —
"Work is bread and bread is living" —
Through the long celestial day.
 Contemporary Verse   *Scudder Middleton*

70   *A Dog*

SO, back again?
       — And is your errand done,
Unfailing one?
How quick the gray world, at your morning look,
Turns wonder-book!

Come in, — O guard and guest.
Come, O you breathless from a life-long quest; —
Search here my heart; and if a comfort be,
Ah, comfort me!
You eloquent one, you best
Of all diviners, so to trace
The weather-gleams upon a face;
With wordless, querying paw,
Adventuring the law!
You shaggy Loveliness,
What call was it? — What dream beyond a guess,
Lured you, gray ages back,
From that lone bivouac
Of the wild pack? —
Was it your need? — Or ours, the calling trail
Of faith that should not fail? —
Of hope dim understood? —
That you should follow our poor humanhood,
Only because you would!
To search and circle, — follow and outstrip,
Men and their fellowship;
And keep your heart no less,
Your back-and-forth of hope and wistfulness,
Through all world-weathers and against all odds!
Can you forgive us, now, —
Your fallen gods?

Josephine Preston Peabody
The Poetry Review of America

71   *The Night Court*

"CALL Rose Costara!"
            Insolent, she comes.
The watchers, practised, keen, turn down their thumbs.
The walk, the talk, the face, — that sea-shell tint, —
It is old stuff; they read her like coarse print.
Here is no hapless innocence waylaid.
This is a stolid worker at her trade.
Listening, she yawns; half smiling, undismayed,
Shrugging a little at the law's delay,
Bored and impatient to be on her way.
It is her eighth conviction. Out beyond the rail
A lady novelist in search of types turns pale.
She meant to write of them just as she found them,
And with no tears or maudlin glamour round them,
In forceful, virile words, harsh, true words, without shame,
Calling an ugly thing, boldly, an ugly name;
Sympathy, velvet glove, on purpose, iron hand.
But *eighth conviction!* All the phrases she had planned
Fail; "sullen," "vengeful," no, she is n't that.
No, the pink face beneath the hectic hat
Gives back her own aghast and sickened stare
With a detached and rather cheerful air,
And then the little novelist sees red.
From her chaste heart all clemency is fled.
"Oh, loathsome! venomous! Off with her head!
Call Rose Costara!" But before you stop,
And shelve your decent rage,
            Let's call the cop.

Let's call the plain-clothes cop who brought her in.
The weary-eyed night watchman of the law,
A shuffling person with a hanging jaw,
Loose-lipped and sallow, rather vague of chin,
Comes rubber-heeling at his Honor's rap.
He set and baited and then sprung the trap —
The *trap* — by his unsavory report.
Let's ask him why — but first
    Let's call the court.

Not only the grim figure in the chair,
Sphinx-like above the waste and wreckage there,
Skeptical, weary of a retold tale,
But the whole humming hive, the false, the frail, —
An old young woman with a weasel face,
A lying witness waiting in his place,
Two ferret lawyers nosing out a case,
Reporters questioning a Mexican,
Sobbing her silly heart out for her man,
Planning to feature her, "lone desperate, pretty," —
Yes, call the court.   But wait!
    Let's call the city.

Call the community!   Call up, call down,
Call all the speeding, mad, unheeding town!
Call rags and tags and then call velvet gown!
Go, summon them from tenements and clubs,
On office floors and over steaming tubs!
Shout to the boxes and behind the scenes,
Then to the push-carts and the limousines!
Arouse the lecture-room, the cabaret!

Confound them with a trumpet-blast and say,
"Are you so dull, so deaf and blind indeed,
That you mistake the harvest for the seed?"
Condemn them for — but stay!
                Let's call the code —

That facile thing they've fashioned to their mode:
Smug sophistries that smother and befool,
That numb and stupefy; that clumsy thing
That measures mountains with a three-foot rule,
And plumbs the ocean with a pudding-string —
The little, brittle code.   Here is the root,
Far out of sight, and buried safe and deep,
And Rose Costara is the bitter fruit.
On every limb and leaf, death, ruin, creep.

So, lady novelist, go home again.
Rub biting acid on your little pen.
Look back and out and up and in, and then
Write that it is no job for pruning-shears.
Tell them to dig for years and years and years
The twined and twisted roots.   Blot out the page;
Invert the blundering order of the age;
Reverse the scheme: the last shall be the first.
Summon the system, starting with the worst —
The lying, dying code!   On, down the line,
The city and the court, the cop.   Assign
The guilt, the blame, the shame!   Sting, lash, and spur!
Call each and all!   Call us!   And *then* call her!
The Century Magazine   Ruth Comfort Mitchell

72 Guns as Keys: and the Great Gate Swings

PART I

DUE East, far West. Distant as the nests of the opposite winds. Removed as fire and water are, as the clouds and the roots of the hills, as the wills of youth and age. Let the key-guns be mounted, make a brave show of waging war, and pry off the lid of Pandora's box once more. Get in at any cost and let out at little, so it seems, but wait — wait — there is much to follow through the Great Gate!

They do not see things in quite that way, on this bright November day, with sun flashing, and waves splashing, up and down Chesapeake Bay. On shore, all the papers are running to press with huge headlines: "Commodore Perry Sails." Dining-tables buzz with travellers' tales of old Japan culled from Dutch writers. But we are not like the Dutch. No shutting the stars and stripes up on an island. Pooh! We must trade wherever we have a mind. Naturally!

The wharves of Norfolk are falling behind, becoming smaller, confused with the warehouses and the trees. On the impetus of the strong South breeze, the paddle-wheel steam frigate *Mississippi* of the United States Navy, sails down the flashing bay. Sails away, and steams away, for her furnaces are burning, and her paddle-wheels turning, and all her sails are set and full. Pull, men, to the old chorus:

"A Yankee ship sails down the river,
  Blow, boys, blow;
Her masts and spars they shine like silver,
  Blow, my bully boys, blow."

But what is the use? That plaguey brass band blares out with "The Star-Spangled Banner," and you cannot hear the men because of it. Which is a pity, thinks the Commodore, in his cabin, studying the map, and marking stepping-stones: Madeira, Cape Town, Mauritius, Singapore, nice firm stepping-places for seven-league boots. Flag-stones up and down a hemisphere.

My! How she throws the water off from her bows, and how those paddle-wheels churn her along at the rate of seven good knots! You are a proud lady, *Mrs. Mississippi*, curtseying down Chesapeake Bay, all a-flutter with red, white and blue ribbons.

At Mishiwa in the Province of Kai,
Three men are trying to measure a pine tree
By the length of their outstretched arms.
Trying to span the bole of a huge pine tree
By the spread of their lifted arms.
Attempting to compress its girth
Within the limit of their extended arms.
Beyond, Fuji,
Majestic, inevitable,
Wreathed over by wisps of cloud.
The clouds draw about the mountain,
But there are gaps.
The men reach about the pine tree,
But their hands break apart;

The rough bark escapes their hand-clasps;
The tree is unencircled.
Three men are trying to measure the stem of a gigantic
    pine tree,
With their arms,
At Mishiwa in the Province of Kai.

Furnaces are burning good Cumberland coal at the rate of twenty-six tons *per diem*, and the paddle-wheels turn round and round in an iris of spray. She noses her way through a wallowing sea; foots it, bit by bit, over the slanting wave slopes; pants along, thrust forward by her breathing furnaces, urged ahead by the wind draft flattening against her taut sails.

The Commodore, leaning over the taffrail, sees the peak of Madeira swept up out of the haze. The *Mississippi* glides into smooth water, and anchors under the lee of the "Desertas."

Ah! the purple bougainvillia! And the sweet smells of the heliotrope and geranium hedges! Ox-drawn sledges clattering over cobbles — what a fine pause in an endless voyaging. Stars and stripes demanding five hundred tons of coal, ten thousand gallons of water, resting for a moment on a round stepping-stone, with the drying sails slatting about in the warm wind.

"Get out your accordion, Jim, and give us the 'Sewanee River' to show those Dagos what a tune is. Pipe up with the chorus, boys. Let her go."

The green water flows past Madeira. Flows under the paddle-boards, making them clip and clap. The green water washes along the sides of the Commodore's steam flagship and passes away to leeward.

"Hitch up your trousers, Black Face, and do a hornpipe. It's a fine quiet night for a double shuffle. Keep her going, Jim. Louder. That's the ticket. Gosh, but you can spin, Blackey!"

The road is hilly
Outside the Tiger Gate,
And striped with shadows from a bow moon
Slowly sinking to the horizon.
The roadway twinkles with the bobbing of paper lanterns,
Melon-shaped, round, oblong,
Lighting the steps of those who pass along it;
And there is a sweet singing of many *semi*,
From the cages which an insect seller
Carries on his back.

Westward of the Canaries, in a wind-blazing sea. Engineers, there, extinguish the furnaces; carpenters, quick, your screwdrivers and mallets, and unship the paddle-boards. Break out her sails, quartermasters, the wind will carry her faster than she can steam, for the trades have her now, and are whipping her along in fine clipper style. Key-guns, your muzzles shine like basalt above the tumbling waves. Polished basalt cameoed upon malachite. Yankee-doodle-dandy! A fine upstanding ship, clouded with canvas, slipping along like a trotting filly out of the Commodore's own stables. White sails and sailors, blue-coated officers, and red in a star sparked through the claret decanter on the Commodore's luncheon table.

The Commodore is writing to his wife, to be posted

at the next stopping place. Two years is a long time to be upon the sea.

> Nigi-oi of Matsuba-ya
> Celebrated oiran,
> Courtesan of unrivalled beauty,
> The great silk mercer, Mitsui,
> Counts himself a fortunate man
> As he watches her parade in front of him
> In her robes of glazed blue silk
> Embroidered with singing nightingales.
> He puffs his little silver pipe
> And arranges a fold of her dress.
> He parts it at the neck
> And laughs when the falling plum-blossoms
> Tickle her naked breasts.
> The next morning he makes out a bill
> To the Director of the Dutch Factory at Nagasaki
> For three times the amount of the goods
> Forwarded that day in two small junks
> In the care of a trusted clerk.

The Northeast trades have smoothed away into hot, blue doldrums. Paddle-wheels to the rescue. Thank God, we live in an age of invention. What air there is, is dead ahead. The deck is a bed of cinders, we wear a smoke cloud like a funeral plume. Funeral — of whom? Of the little heathens inside the Gate? Wait! Wait! These monkey-men have got to trade, Uncle Sam has laid his plans with care, see those black guns sizzling there. "It's deuced hot," says a lieutenant, "I wish I could look in at a hop in Newport this evening."

The one hundred and sixty streets in the Sanno quarter
Are honey-gold,
Honey-gold from the gold-foil screens in the houses,
Honey-gold from the fresh yellow mats;
The lintels are draped with bright colors,
And from eaves and poles
Red and white paper lanterns
Glitter and swing.
Through the one hundred and sixty decorated streets
    of the Sanno quarter,
Trails the procession,
With a bright slowness,
To the music of flutes and drums.
Great white sails of cotton
Belly out along the honey-gold streets.
Sword bearers,
Spear bearers,
Mask bearers,
Grinning masks of mountain genii,
And a white cock on a drum
Above a purple sheet.
Over the flower hats of the people,
Shines the sacred palanquin,
"Car of gentle motion,"
Upheld by fifty men,
Stalwart servants of the god,
Bending under the weight of mirror-black lacquer,
Of pillars and roof-tree
Wrapped in chased and gilded copper.
Portly silk tassels sway to the marching of feet,
Wreaths of gold and silver flowers
Shoot sudden scintillations at the gold-foil screens.

The golden phœnix on the roof of the palanquin
Spreads its wings,
And seems about to take flight
Over the one hundred and sixty streets
Straight into the white heart
Of the curved blue sky.
Six black oxen,
With white and red trappings,
Draw platforms on which are musicians, dancers, actors,
Who posture and sing,
Dance and parade,
Up and down the honey-gold streets,
To the sweet playing of flutes,
And the ever-repeating beat of heavy drums,
To the constant banging of heavily beaten drums,
To the insistent repeating rhythm of beautiful great
    drums.

Across the equator and panting down to Saint Helena, trailing smoke like a mourning veil. Jamestown jetty, and all the officers in the ship making at once for Longwood. Napoleon! Ah, tales — tales — with nobody to tell them. A bronze eagle caged by floating wood-work. A heart burst with beating on a flat drop-curtain of sea and sky. Nothing now but pigs in a sty. Pigs rooting in the Emperor's bedroom. God be praised, we have a plumed smoking ship to take us away from this desolation.

      "Boney was a warrior
        Away-i-oh;
      Boney was a warrior,
        John François."

"Oh, shut up, Jack, you make me sick. Those pigs are like worms eating a corpse. Bah!"

The ladies,
Wistaria Blossom, Cloth-of-Silk, and Deep Snow,
With their ten attendants,
Are come to Asakusa
To gaze at peonies.
To admire crimson-carmine peonies,
To stare in admiration at bomb-shaped, white and
    sulphur peonies,
To caress with a soft finger
Single, rose-flat peonies,
Tight, incurved, red-edged peonies,
Spin-wheel circle, amaranth peonies.
To smell the acrid pungence of peony blooms,
And dream for months afterwards
Of the temple garden at Asakusa,
Where they walked together
Looking at peonies.

The Gate! The Gate! The far-shining Gate! Pat your guns and thank your stars you have not come too late. The Orient's a sleepy place, as all globe-trotters say. We'll get there soon enough, my lads, and carry it away. That's a good enough song to round the Cape with, and there's the Table Cloth on Table Mountain and we've drawn a bead over half the curving world. Three cheers for Old Glory, fellows.

  A Daimino's procession
  Winds between two green hills,

A line of thin, sharp, shining, pointed spears
Above red coats
And yellow mushroom hats.
A man leading an ox
Has cast himself upon the ground,
He rubs his forehead in the dust,
While his ox gazes with wide, moon eyes
At the glittering spears
Majestically parading
Between two green hills.

Down, down, down, to the bottom of the map; but we must up again, high on the other side. America, sailing the seas of a planet to stock the shop counters at home. Commerce-raiding a nation; pulling apart the curtains of a temple and calling it trade. Magnificent mission! Every shop-till in every by-street will bless you. Force the shut gate with the muzzles of your black cannon. Then wait — wait for fifty years — and see who has conquered.

But now the *Mississippi* must brave the Cape, in a crashing of bitter seas. The wind blows East, the wind blows West, there is no rest under these clashing clouds. Petrel whirl by like torn newspapers along a street. Albatrosses fly close to the mast-heads. Dread purrs over this stormy ocean, and the smell of the water is the dead, oozing dampness of tombs.

Tiger rain on the temple bridge of carved greenstone,
Slanting tiger lines of rain on the lichened lanterns of
    the gateway,
On the stone statues of mythical warriors.

Striped rain making the bells of the pagoda roofs flutter,
Tiger-footing on the bluish stones of the courtyard,
Beating, snapping, on the cheese-rounds of open umbrellas,
Licking, tiger-tongued, over the straw mat which a pilgrim wears upon his shoulders,
Gnawing, tiger-toothed, into the paper mask
Which he carries on his back.
Tiger-clawed rain scattering the peach-blossoms,
Tiger tails of rain lashing furiously among the cryptomerias.

"Land — O." Mauritius. Stepping-stone four. The coaling ships have arrived, and the shore is a hive of Negroes, and Malays, and Lascars, and Chinese. The clip and clatter of tongues is unceasing. "What awful brutes!" "Obviously, but the fruits they sell are good." "Food, fellows, bully good food." Yankee money for pine-apples, shaddocks, mangoes. "Who were Paul and Virginia?" "Oh, a couple of spooneys who died here, in a shipwreck, because the lady would n't take off her smock." "I say, Fred, that's a shabby way to put it. You've no sentiment." "Maybe, I don't read much myself, and when I do, I prefer United States, something like old Artemus Ward, for instance." "Oh, dry up, and let's get some donkeys and go for a gallop. We've got to begin coaling to-morrow, remember."

The beautiful dresses,
Blue, Green, Mauve, Yellow;
And the beautiful green pointed hats
Like Chinese porcelains!

See, a band of geisha
Is imitating the state procession of a Corean Ambassador,
Under painted streamers,
On an early afternoon.

The hot sun burns the tar up out of the deck. The paddle-wheels turn, flinging the cupped water over their shoulders. Heat smoulders along the horizon. The shadow of the ship floats off the starboard quarter, floats like a dark cloth on the sea. The watch is pulling on the topsail halliards:

"O Sally Brown of New York City,
Ay, ay, roll and go."

Like a tired beetle, the *Mississippi* creeps over the flat, glass water, creeps on, breathing heavily. Creeps — creeps — and sighs and settles at Pointe de Galle, Ceylon.

Spice islands speckling the Spanish Main. Fairy tales and stolen readings. Saint John's Eve! Midsummer Madness! Here it is all true. But the smell of the spice-trees is not so nice as the smell of new-mown hay on the Commodore's field at Tarrytown. But what can one say to forests of rose-wood, satin-wood, ebony! To the talipot tree, one leaf of which can cover several people with its single shade. Trade! Trade! Trade in spices for an earlier generation. We dream of lacquers and precious stones. Of spinning telegraph wires across painted fans. Ceylon is an old story, ours will be the glory of more important conquests.

But wait — wait. No one is likely to force the Gate.

The smoke of golden Virginia tobacco floats through the blue palms. "You say you killed forty elephants with this rifle!" "Indeed, yes, and a trifling bag, too."

> Down the ninety mile rapids
> Of the Heaven Dragon River,
> He came,
> With his bowmen,
> And his spearmen,
> Borne in a gilded palanquin,
> To pass the Winter in Yedo
> By the Shogun's decree.
> To pass the Winter idling in the Yoshiwara,
> While his bowmen and spearmen
> Gamble away their rusted weapons
> Every evening
> At the Hour of the Cock.

Her Britannic Majesty's frigate *Cleopatra* salutes the *Mississippi* as she sails into the harbor of Singapore. Vessels galore choke the wharves. From China, Siam, Malaya; Sumatra, Europe, America. This is the bargain counter of the East. Goods — Goods, dumped ashore to change boats and sail on again. Oaths and cupidity; greasy clothes and greasy dollars wound into turbans. Opium and birds'-nests exchanged for teas, cassia, nankeens; gold thread bartered for Brummagem buttons. Pocket knives told off against teapots. Lots and lots of cheap damaged porcelains, and trains of silken bales awaiting advantageous sales to Yankee merchantmen. The figurehead of the *Mississippi* should be a beneficent angel. With her guns to persuade, she should lay the foundation of such a market on the shores of Japan. "We will do what we can," writes the Commodore, in his cabin.

> Outside the drapery shop of Taketani Sabai,
> Strips of dried cloth are hanging out to dry.
> Fine Arimitsu cloth,
> Fine blue and white cloth,
> Falling from a high staging,
> Falling like falling water,
> Like blue and white unbroken water
> Sliding over a high cliff,
> Like the Ono Fall on the Kisokaido Road.
> Outside the shop of Taketani Sabai,
> They have hung the fine dyed cloth
> In strips out to dry.

Romance and heroism; and all to make one dollar two. Through grey fog and fresh blue breezes, through heat, and sleet, and sheeted rain. For centuries men have pursued the will-o'-the-wisp — trade. And they have got — what? All civilization weighed in twopenny scales and fastened with string. A sailing planet packed in a dry-goods box. Knocks, and shocks, and blocks of extended knowledge, contended for and won. Cloves and nutmegs, and science stowed among the grains. Your gains are not in silver, mariners, but in the songs of violins, and the thin voices whispering through printed books.

"It looks like a dinner-plate," thinks the officer of the watch, as the *Mississippi* sails up the muddy river to Canton, with the Dragon's Cave Fort on one side, and the Girl's Shoe Fort on the other.

The Great Gate looms in a distant mist, and the anchored squadron waits and rests, but its coming is as certain as the equinoxes, and the lightning bolts of its guns are ready to tear off centuries like husks of corn.

The Commodore sips bottled water from Saratoga, and makes out a report for the State Department. The men play pitch-and-toss, and the officers poker, and the betting gives heavy odds against the little monkey-men.

    On the floor of the reception room of the Palace
    They have laid a white quilt,
    And on the quilt, two red rugs;
    And they have set up two screens of white paper
    To hide that which should not be seen.
    At the four corners, they have placed lanterns,
    And now they come.
    Six attendants,
    Three to sit on either side of the condemned man,
    Walking slowly.
    Three to the right,
    Three to the left,
    And he between them
    In his dress of ceremony
    With the great wings.
    Shadow wings, thrown by the lantern light,
    Trail over the red rugs to the polished floor,
    Trail away unnoticed,
    For there is a sharp glitter from a dagger
    Borne past the lanterns on a silver tray,
    "O my Master,
    I would borrow your sword,

For it may be a consolation to you
To perish by a sword to which you are accustomed."
Stone, the face of the condemned man,
Stone, the face of the executioner,
And yet before this moment
These were master and pupil,
Honored and according homage,
And this is an act of honorable devotion.
Each face is passive,
Hewed as out of strong stone,
Cold as a statue above a temple porch.
Down slips the dress of ceremony to the girdle.
Plunge the dagger to its hilt.
A trickle of blood runs along the white flesh
And soaks into the girdle silk.
Slowly across from left to right,
Slowly, upcutting at the end,
But the executioner leaps to his feet,
Poises the sword —
Did it flash, hover, descend?
There is a thud, a horrible rolling,
And the heavy sound of a loosened, falling body,
Then only the throbbing of blood
Spurting into the red rugs.
For he who was a man is that thing
Crumpled up on the floor,
Broken, and crushed into the red rugs.
The friend wipes the sword,
And his face is calm and frozen
As a stone statue on a Winter night
Above a temple gateway.

THE GOLDEN TREASURY

PART II

Four vessels giving easily to the low running waves and catspaw breezes of a Summer sea. July, 1853, Mid-Century, but just on the turn. Mid-Century, with the vanishing half fluttering behind on a foam-bubbled wake. Four war ships steering for the "Land of Great Peace," caparisoned in state, cleaving a jewelled ocean to a Dragon Gate. Behind it, the quiet of afternoon. Golden light reflecting from the inner sides of shut portals. War is an old wives' tale, a frail beautiful embroidery of other ages. The panoply of battle fades. Arrows rust in arsenals, spears stand useless on their butts in vestibules. Cannon lie unmounted in castle yards, and rats and snakes make nests in them and rear their young in unmolested satisfaction.

The sun of midsummer lies over the "Land of Great Peace," and behind the shut gate they do not hear the paddle-wheels of distant vessels unceasingly turning and advancing, through the jewelled scintillations of the encircling sea.

Susquehanna and *Mississippi*, steamers, towing *Saratoga* and *Plymouth*, sloops of war. Moving on in the very eye of the wind, with not a snip of canvas upon their slim yards. Fugi! — a point above nothing, for there is a haze. Stop gazing, that is the bugle to clear decks and shot guns. We must be prepared, as we run up the coast straight to the Bay of Yedo. "I say, fellows, those boats think they can catch us, they don't know that this is Yankee steam." Bang! The shore guns are at work. And that smoke-ball would be a rocket at night, but we cannot see the gleam in this sunshine.

Black with people are the bluffs of Uraga, watching the "fire-ships" lipping windless up the bay. Say all the prayers you know, priests of Shinto and Buddha. Ah! The great splashing of the wheels stops, a chain rattles. The anchor drops at the hour of the ape.

A clock on the Commodore's chest of drawers strikes five with a silvery tinkle.

Boats are coming from all directions. Beautiful boats of unpainted wood, broad of beam, with tapering sterns, and clean runs. Swiftly they come, with shouting rowers standing to their oars. The shore glitters with spears and lacquered hats. Compactly the boats advance, and each carries a flag — white-black-white — and the stripes break and blow. But the tow-lines are cast loose when the rowers would make them fast to the "black ships," and those who would climb the chains slip back dismayed, checked by a show of cutlasses, pistols, pikes. "*Naru Hodo!*" This is amazing, unprecedented! Even the Vice Governor, though he boards the *Susquehanna*, cannot see the Commodore. "His High Mighty Mysteriousness, Lord of the Forbidden Interior," remains in his cabin. Extraordinary! Horrible!

Rockets rise from the forts, and their trails of sparks glitter faintly now, and their bombs break in faded colors as the sun goes down.

Bolt the gate, monkey-men, but it is late to begin turning locks so rusty and worn.

Darkness over rice-fields and hills. The Gold Gate hides in shadow. Upon the indigo-dark water, millions of white jelly-fish drift, like lotus-petals over an inland lake. The land buzzes with prayer, low, dim smoke hanging in air; and every hill gashes and glares with shooting fires. The fire-bells are ringing in double time, and a heavy swinging boom clashes from the great bells of temples. Couriers lash their horses, riding furiously to Yedo; junks and scull-boats arrive hourly at Shinagawa with news; runners, bearing dispatches, pant in government offices. The hollow doors of the Great Gate beat with alarms. The charmed Dragon country shakes and trembles. Iyéyoshi, twelfth Shogun of the Tokugawa line, sits in his city. Sits in the midst of one million, two hundred thousand trembling souls, and his mind rolls forward and back like a ball on a circular runway, and finds no goal. Roll, poor distracted mind of a sick man. What can you do but wait, trusting in your Dragon Gate, for how should you know that it is rusted.

But there is a sign over the "black ships." A wedge-shaped tail of blue sparklets, edged with red, trails above them as though a Dragon were pouring violet sulphurous spume from steaming nostrils, and the hulls and rigging are pale, quivering, bright as Taira ghosts on the sea of Nagato.

Up and down, walk sentinels, fore and aft, and at the side gangways. There is a pile of round shot and four stands of grape beside each gun; and carbines, and pistols, and cutlasses, are laid in the boats. Floating arsenals — floating sample-rooms for the wares of a continent, shop-counters, flanked with weapons, adrift among the jelly-fishes.

Eight bells, and the meteor washes away before the wet, white wisps of dawn.

Through the countrysides of the "Land of Great

Peace," flowers are blooming. The greenish-white, sterile blossoms of hydrangeas boom faintly like distant inaudible bombs of color exploding in the woods. Weigelias prick the pink of their slender trumpets against green backgrounds. The fan-shaped leaves of ladies' slippers rustle under cryptomerias.

Midsummer heat curls about the cinnamon-red tree-boles along the Tokaido. The road ripples and glints with the passing to and fro, and beyond, in the roadstead, the "black ships" swing at their anchors and wait.

All up and down the Eastern shore of the bay is a feverish digging, patting, plastering. Forts to be built in an hour to resist the barbarians, if, peradventure, they can. Japan turned to, what will it not do! Fishermen and palanquin-bearers, packhorse-leaders and farm-laborers, even women and children, pat and plaster. Disaster batters at the Dragon Gate. Batters at the doors of Yedo, where Samurai unpack their armour, and whet and feather their arrows.

Daimios smoke innumerable pipes, and drink unnumbered cups of tea, discussing — discussing — "What is to be done?" The Shogun is no Emperor. What shall they do if the "hairy devils" take a notion to go to Kioto! Then indeed would the Tokugawa fall. The prisons are crammed with those who advise opening the Gate. Open the Gate, and let the State scatter like dust to the wind! Absurd! Unthinkable! Suppress the "brocade pictures" of the floating monsters with which book-sellers and picture-shop keepers are delighting and affrighting the populace. Place a ban on speech. Preach, inett Daimios — the Commodore will *not* go to Nagasaki, and the roar of his guns will drown the clattering fall of your Dragon doors if you do not open them in time. East and West, and trade shaded by heroism. Hokusai is dead, but his pupils are lampooning your carpet soldiers. Spare the dynasty — parley, procrastinate. Appoint two Princes to receive the Commodore, at once, since he will not wait over long. At Kurihama, for he must not come to Yedo.

Flip — flap — flutter — flags in front of the Conference House. Built over night, it seems, with unpainted peaked summits of roofs gleaming like ricks of grain. Flip — flutter — flap — variously-tinted flags, in a crescent about nine tall standards whose long scarlet pennons brush the ground. Beat — tap — fill and relapse — the wind pushing against taut white cloth screens, bellying out the Shogun's crest of heart-shaped Asarum leaves in the panels, crumpling them to indefinite figures of scarlet spotting white. Flip — ripple — brighten — over serried ranks of soldiers on the beach. Sword-bearers, spear-bearers, archers, lancers, and those who carry heavy, antiquated match-locks. The block of them five thousand armed men, drawn up in front of a cracking golden door. But behind their bristling spears, the cracks are hidden.

Braying, blasting blares from two brass bands, approaching in glittering boats over glittering water. One is playing the "Overture" from "William Tell," the other, "The Last Rose of Summer," and the way the notes clash, and shock, and shatter, and dissolve, is wonderful to hear. Queer barbarian music, and the monkey-soldiers stand stock still, listening to its reverberation humming in the folded doors of the Great Gate.

Stuff your ears, monkey-soldiers, screw your faces, shudder up and down your spines. Cannon! Cannon! from one of the "black ships." Thirteen thudding explosions, thirteen red dragon tongues, thirteen clouds of smoke like the breath of the mountain gods. Thirteen hammer strokes shaking the Great Gate, and the seams in the metal widen. Open Sesame, shotless guns; and "The Only, High, Grand and Mighty, Invisible Mysteriousness, Chief Barbarian" reveals himself, and steps into his barge.

Up, oars, down; drip — sun-spray — rowlock-rattle. To shore! To shore! Set foot upon the sacred soil of the "Land of Great Peace," with its five thousand armed men doing nothing with their spears and match-locks, because of the genii in the black guns aboard the "black ships."

One hundred marines in a line up the wharf. One hundred sailors, man to man, opposite them. Officers, two deep; and, up the centre — the Procession. Bands together now: "Hail Columbia." Marines in file, sailors after, a staff with the American flag borne by seamen, another with the Commodore's broad pennant. Two boys, dressed for ceremony, carrying the President's letter and credentials in golden boxes. Tall, blue-black negroes on either side of — THE COMMODORE! Walking slowly, gold, blue, steel-glitter, up to the Conference House, walking in state up to an ancient tottering Gate, lately closed securely, but now gaping. Bands, rain your music against this golden barrier, harry the ears of the monkey-men. The doors are ajar, and the Commodore has entered.

Prince of Idzu — Prince of Iwami — in winged dresses of gold brocade, at the end of a red carpet, under violet, silken hangings, under crests of scarlet heart-shaped Asarum leaves, guardians of a scarlet lacquered box, guardians of golden doors, worn thin and bending.

In silence the blue-black negroes advance, and take the golden boxes from the page boys; in silence they open them and unwrap blue velvet coverings. Silently they display the documents to the Prince of Idzu — the Prince of Iwami — motionless, inscrutable — beyond the red carpet.

The vellum crackles as it is unfolded, and the long silk-gold cords of the seals drop their gold tassels to straight glistening inches and swing slowly — gold tassels clock-ticking before a doomed, burnished gate.

The negroes lay the vellum documents upon the scarlet lacquered box; bow, and retire.

"I am desirous that our two countries should trade with each other." Careful letters, carefully traced on rich parchment, and the low sun casts the shadow of the Gate far inland over high hills.

"The letter of the President of the United States will be delivered to the Emperor. Therefore you can now go."

The Commodore, rising: "I will return for the answer during the coming Spring."

But ships are frail, and seas are fickle, one can nail fresh plating over the thin gate before Spring. Prince of Idzu — Prince of Iwami — inscrutable statesmen, insensate idiots, trusting blithely to a lock when the key-guns are trained even now upon it.

Withdraw, Procession. Dip oars back to the "black ships." Slip cables and depart, for day after day will lapse and nothing can retard a coming Spring.

Panic Winter throughout the "Land of Great Peace." Panic, and haste, wasting energies and accomplishing nothing. Kioto has heard, and prays, trembling. Priests at the shrine of Isé whine long slow supplications from dawn to dawn, and through days dropping down again from morning. Iyéyoshi is dead, and Iyésada rules in Yedo; thirteenth Shogun of the Tokugawa. Rules and struggles, rescinds laws, urges reforms; breathless, agitated endeavors to patch and polish where is only corroding and puffed particles of dust.

It is Winter still in the Bay of Yedo, though the plum-trees of Kamata and Kinagawa are white and fluttering.

Winter, with green, high, angular seas. But over the water, far toward China, are burning the furnaces of three great steamers, and four sailing vessels heel over, with decks slanted and sails full and pulling.

"There's a bit of a lop, this morning. Mr. Jones, you'd better take in those royals." ·

"Ay, ay, Sir. Tumble up here, men! Tumble up! Lay aloft and stow royals. Haul out to leeward."

> "To *my*,
>   Ay,
> And we'll *furl*
>   Ay,
> And pay Paddy Doyle for his boots."

"Tauht band — knot away."

Chug! Chug! go the wheels of the consorts, salting smokestacks with whirled spray.

The Commodore lights a cigar, and paces up and

down the quarter-deck of the *Powhatan*. "I wonder what the old yellow devils will do," he muses.

Forty feet high, the camellia trees, with hard, green buds unburst. It is early yet for camellias, and the green buds and the glazed green leaves toss frantically in a blustering March wind. Sheltered behind the forty feet high camellia trees, on the hills of Idzu, stand watchmen straining their eyes over a broken dazzle of sea.

Just at the edge of moonlight and sunlight — moon setting; sun rising — they come. Seven war ships heeled over and flashing, dashing through heaped waves, sleeping a moment in hollows leaping over ridges, sweeping forward in a strain of canvas and a train of red-black smoke.

"The fire-ships! The fire-ships!"

Slip the bridles of your horses, messengers, and clatter down the Tokaido; scatter pedestrians, palanquins, slow moving cattle, right and left into the cryptomerias; rattle over bridges, spatter dust into shop-windows. To Yedo! To Yedo! For Spring is here, and the fire-ships have come!

Seven vessels, flying the stars and stripes, three more shortly to join them, with ripe, fruit-bearing guns pointed inland.

Princes evince doubt, distrust. Learning must beat learning. Appoint a Professor of the University. Delay, prevaricate. How long can the play continue? Hayashi, learned scholar of Confucius and Mencius — he shall confer with the Barbarians at Uraga. Shall he! Word comes that the Mighty Chief of Ships will not go to

Uraga. Steam is up, and — Horror! Consternation! The squadron moves toward Yedo! Sailors, midshipmen, lieutenants pack yards and cross-trees, seeing temple gates, castle towers, flowered pagodas, and look-outs looming distantly clear, and the Commodore on deck can hear the slow booming of the bells from the temples of Shiba and Asakusa.

You must capitulate, great Princes of a quivering Gate. Say Yokohama, and the Commodore will agree, for they must not come to Yedo.

Rows of japonicas in full bloom outside the Conference House. Flags and streamers, and musicians and pikemen. Five hundred officers, seamen, marines, and the Commodore following in his white-painted gig. A jig of fortune indeed, with a sailor and a professor manœuvring for terms, chess-playing each other in a game of future centuries.

The Americans bring presents. Presents now, to be bought hereafter. Goodwill, to head long bills of imports. Occidental mechanisms to push the Orient into limbo. Fox-moves of interpreters, and Pandora's box with a contents rated far too low.

Round and round goes the little train on its circular railroad, at twenty miles an hour, with grave dignitaries seated on its roof. Smiles, gestures, at messages running over wire, a mile away. Touch the harrows, the plows, the flails, and shudder at the "spirit pictures" of the daguerreotype machine. These Barbarians have harnessed gods and dragons. They build boats which will not sink, and tinker little gold wheels till they follow the swinging of the sun.

Run to the Conference House. See, feel, listen. And

shrug deprecating shoulders at the glisten of silk and lacquer given in return. What are cups cut out of conch-shells, and red-dyed figured crêpe, to railroads, and burning engines!

Go on board the "black ships" and drink mint juleps and brandy smashes, and click your tongues over sweet puddings. Offer the strangers pickled plums, sugared fruits, candied walnuts. Bruit the news far inland through the mouths of countrymen. Who thinks of the Great Gate! Its portals are pushed so far back that the shining edges of them can scarcely be observed. The Commodore has never swerved a moment from his purpose, and the dragon mouths of his guns have conquered without the need of a single powder-horn.

The Commodore writes in his cabin. Writes an account of what he has done.

The sands of centuries run fast, one slides, and another, each falling into a smother of dust.

A locomotive in pay for a Whistler; telegraph wires buying a revolution; weights and measures and Audubon's birds in exchange for fear. Yellow monkey-men leaping out of Pandora's box, shaking the rocks of the Western coastline. Golden California bartering panic for prints. The dressing-gowns of a continent won at the cost of security. Artists and philosophers lost in the hour-glass and pouring through an open Gate.

Ten ships sailing for China on a fair May wind. Ten ships sailing from one world into another, but never again into the one they left. Two years and a tip-turn is accomplished. Over the globe and back, Rip Van Winkle ships. Slip into your docks in Newport, in Norfolk, in Charlestown. You have blown off the locks of the East, and what is coming will come.

POSTLUDE

In the Castle moat, lotus flowers are blooming,
They shine with the light of an early moon
Brightening above the Castle towers.
They shine in the dark circles of their unreflecting leaves.
Pale blossoms,
Pale towers,
Pale moon,
Deserted ancient moat
About an ancient stronghold,
Your bowmen are departed,
Your strong walls are silent,
Their only echo
A croaking of frogs.
Frogs croaking at the moon
In the ancient moat
Of an ancient, crumbling Castle.

1903. JAPAN

The high cliff of the Kegon waterfall, and a young man carving words on the trunk of a tree. He finishes, pauses an instant, and then leaps into the foam-cloud rising from below. But, on the tree-trunk, the newly-cut words blaze white and hard as though set with diamonds:
"How mightily and steadily go Heaven and Earth! How infinite the duration of Past and Present! Try to measure this vastness with five feet. A word explains the Truth of the whole Universe — *unknowable*. To cure my agony I have decided to die. Now, as I stand

on the crest of this rock, no uneasiness is left in me. For the first time I know that extreme pessimism and extreme optimism are one."

1903.   AMERICA

"Nocturne — Blue and silver — Battersea Bridge.
Nocturne — Grey and Silver — Chelsea Embankment.
Variations in Violet and Green."

Pictures in a glass-roofed gallery, and all day long the throng of people is so great that one can scarcely see them. Debits — credits? Flux and flow through a wide gateway. Occident — Orient — after fifty years.
The Seven Arts *Amy Lowell*

73   *The Field of Glory*

WAR shook the land where Levi dwelt,
   And fired the dismal wrath he felt,
That such a doom was ever wrought
As his, to toil while others fought;
To toil, to dream — and still to dream,
With one day barren as another;
To consummate, as it would seem,
The dry despair of his old mother.

Far off one afternoon began
The sound of man destroying man;
And Levi, sick with nameless rage,
Condemned again his heritage,

And sighed for scars that might have come,
And would, if once he could have sundered
Those harsh, inhering claims of home
That held him while he cursed and wondered.

Another day, and then there came,
Rough, bloody, ribald, hungry, lame,
But yet themselves, to Levi's door,
Two remnants of the day before.
They laughed at him and what he sought;
They jeered him, and his painful acre;
But Levi knew that they had fought,
And left their manners to their Maker.

That night, for the grim widow's ears,
With hopes that hid themselves in fears,
He told of arms, and featly deeds,
Whereat one leaps the while he reads,
And said he'd be no more a clown,
While others drew the breath of battle.
The mother looked him up and down,
And laughed — a scant laugh with a rattle.

She told him what she found to tell,
And Levi listened, and heard well
Some admonitions of a voice
That left him no cause to rejoice.
He sought a friend, and found the stars,
And prayed aloud that they should aid him;
But they said not a word of wars,
Or of a reason why God made him.

And who's of this or that estate
We do not wholly calculate,
When baffling shades that shift and cling
Are not without their glimmering;
When even Levi, tired of faith,
Beloved of none, forgot by many,
Dismissed as an inferior wraith,
Reborn may be as great as any.
The Outlook　　　　　　　*Edwin Arlington Robinson*

74　　　　　　*Fight*

The Tale of a Gunner at Plattsburgh, 1814 [1]

JOCK bit his mittens off and blew his thumbs;
　He scraped the fresh sleet from the frozen sign:
MEN WANTED — VOLUNTEERS.　Like gusts of brine
　　　　He whiffed deliriums
Of sound — the droning roar of rolling rolling drums
And shrilling fifes, like needles in his spine,
And drank, blood-bright from sunrise and wild shore,
　　　　The wine of war.

With ears and eyes he drank and dizzy brain
Till all the snow danced red.　The little shacks

[1] In the naval battle of Plattsburgh, the American commander "Macdonough himself worked like a common sailor, in pointing and handling a favorite gun. While bending over to sight it, a round shot cut in two the spanker boom, which fell on his head and struck him senseless for two or three minutes; he then leaped to his feet and continued as before, *when a shot took off the head of the captain of the gun crew and drove it in his face with such force as to knock him to the other side of the deck.*" — From "The Naval War of 1812," by Theodore Roosevelt.

That lined the road of muffled hackmatacks
      Were roofed with the red stain,
Which spread in reeling rings on icy-blue Champlain
And splotched the sky like daubs of sealing-wax,
That darkened when he winked, and when he stared
      Caught fire and flared.

MEN WANTED — VOLUNTEERS! The village street,
Topped by the slouching store and slim flagpole,
Loomed grand as Rome to his expanding soul;
      Grandly the rhythmic beat
Of feet in file and flags and fifes and filing feet,
The roar of brass and unremitting roll
Of drums and drums bewitched his boyish mood —
      Till he hallooed.

His strident echo stung the lake's wild dawn
And startled him from dreams. Jock rammed his cap
And rubbed a numb ear with the furry flap,
      Then bolted like a faun,
Bounding through shin-deep sleigh-ruts in his shaggy
      brawn,
Blowing white frost-wreaths from red mouth agap
Till, in a gabled porch beyond the store,
      He burst the door:

"Mother!" he panted. "Hush! Your pa ain't up;
He's worser since this storm. What's struck ye so?"
"It's volunteers!" The old dame stammered "Oh!"
      And stopped, and stirred her sup
Of morning tea, and stared down in the trembling cup.

"They're musterin' on the common now." "I know,"
She nodded feebly; then with sharp surmise
      She raised her eyes:

She raised her eyes, and poured their light on him
Who towered glowing there — bright lips apart,
Cap off, and brown hair tousled. With quick smart
      She felt the room turn dim
And seemed she heard, far off, a sound of cherubim
Soothing the sudden pain about her heart.
How many a lonely hour of after-woe
      She saw him so!

"Jock!" And once more the white lips murmured "Jock!"
Her fingers slipped; the spilling teacup fell
And shattered, tinkling — but broke not the spell.
      His heart began to knock,
Jangling the hollow rhythm of the ticking clock.
"Mother, it's fight, and men are wanted!" "Well,
Ah well, it's men may kill us women's joys,
      It's men — not boys!"

"I'm seventeen! I guess that seventeen —"
"My little Jock!" "Little! I'm six-foot-one.
(Scorn twitched his lip.) You saw me, how I skun
      The town last Hallowe'en
At wrastlin'." (Now the mother shifted tack.) "But
      Jean?
You won't be leavin' *Jean?*" "I guess a gun
Won't rattle *her*." He laughed, and turned his head.
      His face grew red.

"But if it does — a gal don't understand:
It's fight!"   "Jock, boy, your pa can't last much more,
And who's to mind the stock — to milk and chore?"
      Jock frowned and gnawed his hand.
"Mother, it's *men* must mind the stock — our own born
      land,
And lick the invaders."   Slowly in the door
Stubbed the old, worn-out man.   "Woman, let be!
      It's liberty:

"It's struck him like fork-lightnin' in a pine.
I felt it, too, like that in seventy-six;
And now, if 't wa'n't for creepin' pains and cricks
      And this one leg o' mine,
I'd holler young Jerusalem like him, and jine
The fight; but fight don't come from burnt-out wicks;
It comes from fire."   "Mebbe," she said, "it comes
      From fifes and drums."

"Dad, all the boys are down from the back hills.
The common's cacklin' like hell's cocks and hens;
There's swords and muskets stacked in the cow-pens
      And knapsacks in the mills;
They say at Isle aux Noix Redcoats are holding drills,
And we're to build a big fleet at Vergennes.
Dad, can't I go?"   "I reckon you're a man:
      Of course you can.

"I'll do the chores to home, you do 'em *thar!*"
"Dad!" — "Lad!"   The men gripped hands and gazed
      upon
The mother, when the door flew wide.   There shone
      A young face like a star,

A gleam of bitter-sweet 'gainst snowy islands far,
A freshness, like the scent of cinnamon,
Tingeing the air with ardor and bright sheen.
      Jock faltered: "Jean!"

"Jock, don't you hear the drums? I dreamed all night
I heard 'em, and they woke me in black dark.
Quick, ain't you comin'? Can't you hear 'em? Hark!
      The men-folks are to fight.
I wish I was a man!" Jock felt his throat clutch tight.
"Men-folks!" It lit his spirit like a spark
Flashing the pent gunpowder of his pride.
      "Come on!" he cried.

"Here — wait!" The old man stumped to the back wall
And handed down his musket. "You'll want this;
And mind what game you're after, and don't miss.
      Good-by: I guess that's all
For now. Come back and get your duds." Jock, looming tall
Beside his glowing sweetheart, stooped to kiss
The little shrunken mother. Tiptoe she rose
      And clutched him — close.

In both her twisted hands she held his head
Clutched in the wild remembrance of dim years —
A baby head, suckling, half dewed with tears;
      A tired boy abed
By candlelight; a laughing face beside the red
Log-fire; a shock of curls beneath her shears —
The bright hair falling. Ah, she tried to smother
      Her wild thoughts — "Mother!

"Mother!" he stuttered. "Baby Jock!" she moaned
And looked far in his eyes. — And he was gone.
The porch door banged. Out in the blood-bright dawn
      All that she once had owned —
Her heart's proud empire — passed, her life's dream sank
      unthroned.
With hands still reached, she stood there staring, wan.
"Hark, woman!" said the bowed old man. "What's
      tolling?"
      Drums — drums were rolling.

II

Shy wings flashed in the orchard, *glitter, glitter;*
Blue wings bloomed soft through blossom-colored leaves,
And *Phœbe! Phœbe!* whistled from gray eaves
      Through water-shine and twitter
And spurt of flamey green. All bane of earth and bitter
Took life and tasted sweet at the glad reprieves
Of Spring, save only in an old dame's heart
      That grieved apart.

Crook-back and small, she poled the big wellsweep:
Creak went the pole; the bucket came up brimming.
On the bright water lay a cricket swimming
      Whose brown legs tried to leap
But, draggling, twitched and foundered in the circling
      deep.
The old dame gasped; her thin hand snatched him, skim-
      ming.
"Dear Lord, he's drowned," she mumbled with dry lips;
      "The ships! the ships!"

Gently she laid him in the sun and dried
The little dripping body.   Suddenly
Rose-red gleamed through the budding apple tree
      And "Look! a letter!" cried
A laughing voice, "and lots of news for us inside!"
"How's that, Jean? News from Jock! Where — where
      is he?"
"Down in Vergennes — the ship-yards." "Ships! Ah, no!
      It can't be so."

"He's goin' to fight with guns and be a tar.
See here: he's wrote himself. The post was late.
He could n't write before. The ship is great!
      She's built, from keel to spar,
And called *the Saratoga;* and Jock's got a scar
Already —" "Scar?" the mother quavered. "Wait,"
Jean rippled, "let me read." "Quick, then, my dear,
      He'll want to hear —

"Jock's pa: I guess we'll find him in the yard.
He ain't scarce creepin' round these days, poor Dan!"
She gripped Jean's arm and stumbled as they ran,
      And stopped once, breathing hard.
Around them chimney-swallows skimmed the sheep-
      cropped sward
And yellow hornets hummed. The sick old man
Stirred at their steps, and muttered from deep muse:
      "Well, ma; what news?"

"From Jockie — there's a letter!" In his chair
The bowed form sat bolt upright. "What's he say?"
"He's wrote to Jean. I guess it's boys their way
      To think old folks don't care

For letters." "Girl, read out." Jean smoothed her
      wilding hair
And sat beside them. Out of the blue day
A golden robin called; across the road
      A heifer lowed;

And old ears listened while youth read: "'Friend Jean,
Vergennes: here's where we've played a Yankee trick.
I'm layin' in my bunk by Otter Crick
      And scribblin' you this mean
Scrawl for to tell the news — what-all I've heerd and seen:
Jennie, we've built a ship, and built her slick —
A swan! — a seven hundred forty tonner,
      And I'm first gunner.

"'You ought to seen us launch her t'other day!
Tell dad we've christened her for a fight of hisn
He fought at Saratoga. Now just listen!
      She's twice as big, folks say,
As Perry's ship that took the prize at Put-in Bay;
Yet forty days ago, hull, masts and mizzen,
The whole of her was growin', live and limber,
      In God's green timber.

"'I helped to fell her main-mast back in March.
The woods was snowed knee-deep. She was a wonder:
A straight white pine. She fell like roarin' thunder
      And left a blue-sky arch
Above her, bustin' all to kindlin's a tall larch. —
Mebbe the scart jack-rabbits skun from under!
Us boys hoorayed, and me and every noodle
      Yelled Yankee-Doodle!

"'My, how we haw'd and gee'd the big ox-sledges
Haulin' her long trunk through the hemlock dells,
A-bellerin' to the tinkle-tankle bells,
    And blunted our ax edges
Hackin' new roads of ice 'longside the rocky ledges.
We stalled her twice, but gave the oxen spells
And yanked her through at last on the home-clearin' —
    Lord, wa'n't we cheerin'!

"'Since then I've seen her born, as you might say:
Born out of fire and water and men's sweatin',
Blast-furnace rairin' and red anvils frettin'
    And sawmills, night and day,
Screech-owlin' like 't was Satan's rumhouse run away
Smellin' of tar and pitch. But I'm forgettin'
The man that's primed her guns and paid her score:
    The Commodore.

"'Macdonough — he's her master, and she knows
His voice, like he was talkin' to his hound.
There ain't a man of her but ruther 'd drown
    Than tread upon his toes;
And yet with his red cheeks and twinklin' eyes, a rose
Ain't friendlier than his looks be. When he's round,
He makes you feel like yo 're a gentleman
    American.

"'But I must tell you how we're hidin' here.
This Otter Crick is like a crook-neck jug,
And we're inside. The Redcoats want to plug
    The mouth, and cork our beer;
So last week Downie sailed his British lake fleet near

To fill our channel, but us boys had dug
Big shore intrenchments, and our batteries
      Stung 'em like bees

"'Till they skedaddled whimperin' up the lake;
But while the shots was flyin', in the scrimmage,
I caught a ball that scotched my livin' image. —
      Now Jean, for Sam Hill's sake,
Don't let-on this to mother, for you know she'd make
A deary-me-in' that would last a grim age.
  'T ain't much, but when a feller goes to war
      What's he go for

"'If 't ain't to fight, and take his chances?'" Jean
Stopped and looked down. The mother did not speak.
"Go on," said the old man. Flush tinged her cheek.
      "Truly I did n't mean —
There ain't much more. He says: 'Goodbye now, little
      queen;
We're due to sail for Plattsburgh this day week.
Meantime I'm hopin' hard and takin' stock.
      Your obedient — Jock.'"

The girl's voice ceased in silence. *Glitter, glitter,*
The shy wings flashed through blossom-colored leaves,
And *Phœbe! Phœbe!* whistled from gray eaves
      Through water-shine and twitter
And spurt of flamey green. But bane of thought is bitter.
The mother's heart spurned May's sweet make-believes,
For there, through falling masts and gaunt ships looming,
      Guns — guns were booming.

III

Plattsburgh — and windless beauty on the bay;
Autumnal morning and the sun at seven:
Southward a wedge of wild ducks in the heaven
      Dwindles, and far away
Dim mountains watch the lake, where lurking for their prey
Lie, with their muzzled thunders and pent levin,
The war-ships — Eagle, Preble, Saratoga,
      Ticonderoga.

And now a little wind from the northwest
Flutters the trembling blue with snowy flecks.
A gunner, on Macdonough's silent decks,
      Peers from his cannon's rest,
Staring beyond the low north headland. Crest on crest
Behind green spruce-tops, soft as wild-fowls' necks,
Glide the bright spars and masts and whitened wales
      Of bellying sails.

Rounding, the British lake-birds loom in view,
Ruffling their wings in silvery arrogance:
Chubb, Linnet, Finch, and lordly Confiance
      Leading with Downie's crew
The line. With long booms swung to starboard they heave to,
Whistling their flock of galleys who advance
Behind, then toward the Yankees, four abreast,
      Tack landward, west.

Landward the watching townsfolk strew the shore;
Mist-banks of human beings blur the bluffs
And blacken the roofs, like swarms of roosting choughs.
      Waiting the cannon's roar
A nation holds its breath for knell of Nevermore
Or peal of life: this hour shall cast the sloughs
Of generations — and one old dame's joy:
      Her gunner boy.

One moment on the quarter deck Jock kneels
Beside his Commodore and fighting squad.
Their heads are bowed, their prayers go up toward God —
      Toward God, to whom appeals
Still rise in pain and mangling wrath from blind ordeals
Of man, still boastful of his brother's blood. —
They stand from prayer. Swift comes and silently
      The enemy.

Macdonough holds his men, alert, devout:
"He that wavereth is like a wave of the sea
Driven with the wind. Behold the ships, that be
      So great, are turned about
Even with a little helm." Jock tightens the blue clout
Around his waist, and watches casually
Close-by a game-cock, in a coop, who stirs
      And spreads his spurs.

Now, bristling near, the British war-birds swoop
Wings, and the Yankee Eagle screams in fire;
The English Linnet answers, aiming higher,
      And *crash* along Jock's poop
Her hurtling shot of iron crackles the game-cock's coop,

Where, lo! the ribald cock, like a town crier
Strutting a gunslide, flaps to the cheering crew —
      Yankee-doodle-doo!

Boys yell, and yapping laughter fills the roar:
"You bet we'll do 'em!" "You're a prophet, cocky!"
"Hooray, old rooster!" "Hip, hip, hip!" cries Jockie.
      Calmly the Commodore
Touches his cannon's fuse and fires a twenty-four.
Smoke belches black. "Huzza! That's blowed 'em
      pockey!"
And Downie's men, like pins before the bowling,
      Fall scatter-rolling.

Boom! flash the long guns, echoed by the galleys.
The Confiance, wind-baffled in the bay
With both her port-bow anchors torn away,
      Flutters, but proudly rallies
To broadside, while her gunboats range the water-alleys.
Then Downie grips Macdonough in the fray,
And double-shotted from his roaring flail
      Hurls the black hail.

The hail turns red, and drips in the hot gloom.
Jock snuffs the reek and spits it from his mouth
And grapples with great winds. The winds blow south,
      And scent of lilac bloom
Steals from his mother's porch in his still sleeping room.
Lilacs! But now it stinks of blood and drouth!
He staggers up, and stares at blinding light:
      "God! This is fight!"

Fight!   The sharp loathing retches in his loins;
He gulps the black air, like a drowner swimming,
Where little round suns in a dance go rimming
    The dark with golden coins;
Round him and round the splintering masts and jangled
        quoins
Reel, rattling, and overhead he hears the hymning —
Lonely and loud — of ululating choirs
    Strangling with wires.

Fight!   But no more the roll of chanting drums,
The fifing flare, the flags, the magic spume
Filling his spirit with a wild perfume;
    Now noisome anguish numbs
His sense, that mocks and leers at monstrous vacuums.
Whang! splits the spanker near him, and the boom
Crushes Macdonough, in a jumbled wreck,
    Stunned on the deck.

No time to glance where wounded leaders lie,
Or think on fallen sparrows in the storm —
Only to fight!   The prone commander's form
    Stirs, rises stumblingly,
And gropes where, under shrieking grape and musketry,
Men's bodies wamble like a mangled swarm
Of bees.   He bends to sight his gun again,
    Bleeding, and then —

Oh, out of void and old oblivion
And reptile slime first rose Apollo's head;
And God in likeness of Himself, 't is said,
    Created such an one,
Now shaping Shakespeare's forehead, now Napoleon,

Various, by infinite invention bred,
In His own image moulding beautiful
    The human skull.

Jock lifts his head; Macdonough sights his gun
To fire — but in his face a ball of flesh,
A whizzing clod, has hurled him in a mesh
    Of tangled rope and tun,
While still about the deck the lubber clod is spun
And, bouncing from the rail, lies in a plesh
Of oozing blood, upstaring eyeless, red —
    A gunner's head.

.   . .   .

Above the ships, enormous from the lake,
Rises a wraith — a phantom dim and gory,
Lifting her wondrous limbs of smoke and glory;
    And little children quake
And lordly nations bow their foreheads for her sake,
And bards proclaim her in their fiery story;
And in her phantom breast, heartless unheeding,
    Hearts — hearts are bleeding.

IV

Macdonough lies with Downie in one land.
Victor and vanquished long ago were peers.
Held in the grip of peace an hundred years,
    England has laid her hand
In ours, and we have held (and still shall hold) the band
That makes us brothers of the hemispheres;
Yea, still shall keep the lasting brotherhood
    Of law and blood.

Yet one whose terror racked us long of yore
Still wreaks upon the world her lawless might:
Out of the deeps again the phantom Fight
      Looms on her wings of war,
Sowing in armed camps and fields her venomed spore,
Embattling monarch's whim against man's right,
Trampling with iron hoofs the blooms of time
      Back in the slime.

We, who from dreams of justice, dearly wrought,
First rose in the eyes of patient Washington,
And through the molten heart of Lincoln won
      To liberty forgot,
Now, standing lone in peace, 'mid titans strange dis-
      traught,
Pray much for patience, more — God's will be done! —
For vision and for power nobly to see
      The world made free.
The Outlook   Percy MacKaye

75   *The Horse Thief*

THERE he moved, cropping the grass at the purple
    canyon's lip.
  His mane was mixed with the moonlight that silvered
    his snow-white side,
For the moon sailed out of a cloud with the wake of a
    spectral ship,
  I crouched and I crawled on my belly, my lariat coil
    looped wide.

Dimly and dark the mesas broke on the starry sky.
  A pall covered every color of their gorgeous glory at noon.
I smelt the yucca and mesquite, and stifled my heart's quick cry,
  And wormed and crawled on my belly to where he moved against the moon!

Some Moorish barb was that mustang's sire. His lines were beyond all wonder.
  From the prick of his ears to the flow of his tail he ached in my throat and eyes.
Steel and velvet grace! As the prophet says, God had "clothed his neck with thunder."
  Oh, marvelous with the drifting cloud he drifted across the skies!

And then I was near at hand, — crouched and balanced, and cast the coil;
  And the moon was smothered in cloud, and the rope through my hands with a rip!
But somehow I gripped and clung, with the blood in my brain aboil, —
  With a turn round the rugged tree-stump there on the purple canyon's lip.

Right into the stars he reared aloft, his red eye rolling and raging.
  He whirled and sunfished and lashed, and rocked the earth to thunder and flame.
He squealed like a regular devil horse. I was haggard and spent and aging —
  Roped clean, but almost storming clear, his fury too fierce to tame.

And I cursed myself for a tenderfoot moon-dazzled to play
    the part,
  But I was doubly desperate then, with the possé pulled
    out from town,
Or I'd never have tried it. I only knew I must get a
    mount and start.
  The filly had snapped her foreleg short. I had had to
    shoot her down.

So there he struggled and strangled, and I snubbed him
    around the tree.
  Nearer, a little near — hoofs planted, and lolling
    tongue —
Till a sudden slack pitched me backward. He reared
    right on top of me.
  Mother of God — that moment! He missed me . . .
    and up I swung.

Somehow, gone daft completely and clawing a bunch of
    his mane,
  As he stumbled and tripped in the lariat, there I was —
    up and astride.
And cursing for seven counties! And the mustang?
    Just insane!
  Crack-bang! went the rope; we cannoned off the tree
    — then — gods, that ride!

A rocket — that's all, a rocket! I dug with my teeth and
    nails.
  Why we never hit even the high spots (though I hardly
    remember things),

But I heard a monstrous booming like a thunder of flapping sails
    When he spread — well, *call* me a liar! — when he spread those wings, those wings!

So white that my eyes were blinded, thick-feathered and wide unfurled,
    They beat the air into billows. We sailed, and the earth was gone.
Canyon and desert and mesa withered below, with the world.
    And then I knew that mustang; for I — was Bellerophon!

Yes, glad as the Greek, and mounted on a horse of the elder gods,
    With never a magic bridle or a fountain-mirror nigh!
My chaps and spurs and holster must have looked it? What's the odds?
    I 'd a leg over lightning and thunder, careering across the sky!

And forever streaming before me, fanning my forehead cool,
    Flowed a mane of molten silver; and just before my thighs
(As I gripped his velvet-muscled ribs, while I cursed myself for a fool),
    The steady pulse of those pinions — their wonderful fall and rise!

The bandanna I bought in Bowie blew loose and whipped from my neck.
    My shirt was stuck to my shoulders and ribboning out behind.

The stars were dancing, wheeling and glancing, dipping
    with smirk and beck.
  The clouds were flowing, dusking and glowing. We
    rode a roaring wind.

We soared through the silver starlight to knock at the
    planets' gates.
  New shimmering constellations came whirling into our
    ken.
Red stars and green and golden swung out of the void
    that waits
  For man's great last adventure; the Signs took shape —
    and then

I knew the lines of that Centaur the moment I saw him
    come!
  The musical-box of the heavens all around us rolled to
    a tune
That tinkled and chimed and trilled with silver sounds
    that struck you dumb,
  As if some archangel were grinding out the music of
    the moon.

Melody-drunk on the Milky Way, as we swept and soared
    hilarious,
  Full in our pathway, sudden he stood — the Centaur
    of the Stars,
Flashing from head and hoofs and breast! I knew him
    for Sagittarius.
  He reared, and bent and drew his bow. He crouched
    as a boxer spars.

Flung back on his haunches, weird he loomed — then
  leapt — and the dim void lightened.
  Old White Wings shied and swerved aside, and fled
    from the splendor-shod.
Through a flashing welter of worlds we charged. I knew
  why my horse was frightened.
  He *had* two faces — a dog's and a man's — that Baby-
    lonian god!

Also, he followed us real as fear. Ping! went an arrow
  past.
  My bronco buck-jumped, humping high. We plunged
    . . . I guess that's all!
I lay on the purple canyon's lip, when I opened my eyes
  at last —
  Stiff and sore and my head like a drum, but I broke no
    bones in the fall.

So you know — and now you may string me up. Such
  was the way you caught me.
  Thank you for letting me tell it straight, though you
    never could greatly care.
For I took a horse that wasn't mine! . . . But there's
  one the heavens brought me,
  And I'll hang right happy, because I know he is wait-
    ing for me up there.

From creamy muzzle to cannon-bone, by God, he's a
  peerless wonder!
  He is steel and velvet and furnace-fire, and death's
    supremest prize;

And never again shall be roped on earth that neck that
    is "clothed with thunder" . . .
  String me up, Dave! Go dig my grave! *I rode him
    across the skies!*
  Poetry: A Magazine of Verse   William Rose Benét

76   *The Bird and the Tree*

BLACKBIRD, blackbird in the cage,
There's something wrong to-night.
Far off the sheriff's footfall dies,
The minutes crawl like last year's flies
Between the bars, and like an age
The hours are long to-night.

The sky is like a heavy lid
Out here beyond the door to-night.
What's that? A mutter down the street.
What's that? The sound of yells and feet.
For what you did n't do or did
You'll pay the score to-night.

No use to reek with reddened sweat,
No use to whimper and to sweat.
They've got the rope; they've got the guns,
They've got the courage and the guns;
And that's the reason why to-night
No use to ask them any more.
They'll fire the answer through the door —
You're out to die to-night.

There where the lonely cross-road lies,
There is no place to make replies;

But silence, inch by inch, is there,
And the right limb for a lynch is there;
And a lean daw waits for both your eyes,
Blackbird.

Perhaps you'll meet again some place.
Look for the mask upon the face;
That's the way you'll know them there —
A white mask to hide the face.
And you can halt and show them there
The things that they are deaf to now,
And they can tell you what they meant —
To wash the blood with blood. But how
If you are innocent?

Blackbird singer, blackbird mute,
They choked the seed you might have found.
Out of a thorny field you go —
For you it may be better so —
And leave the sowers of the ground
To eat the harvest of the fruit,
Blackbird.

Poetry: A Magazine of Verse   *Ridgely Torrence*

77   *1777*

I

The Trumpet-Vine Arbor

THE throats of the little red trumpet-flowers are wide open,
And the clangor of brass beats against the hot sunlight.
They bray and blare at the burning sky.

Red! Red! Coarse notes of red,
Trumpeted at the blue sky.
In long streaks of sound, molten metal,
The vine declares itself.
Clang! — from its red and yellow trumpets;
Clang! — from its long, nasal trumpets,
Splitting the sunlight into ribbons, tattered and shot with noise.
   I sit in the cool arbor, in a green and gold twilight.
It is very still, for I cannot hear the trumpets,
I only know that they are red and open,
And that the sun above the arbor shakes with heat.
My quill is newly mended,
And makes fine-drawn lines with its point.
Down the long white paper it makes little lines,
Just lines — up — down — criss-cross.
My heart is strained out at the pin-point of my quill;
It is thin and writhing like the marks of the pen.
My hand marches to a squeaky tune,
It marches down the paper to a squealing of fifes.
My pen and the trumpet-flowers,
And Washington's armies away over the smoke-tree to the southwest.
"Yankee Doodle," my darling! It is you against the British,
Marching in your ragged shoes to batter down King George.
What have you got in your hat? Not a feather, I wager.
Just a hay-straw, for it is the harvest you are fighting for.
Hay in your hat, and the whites of their eyes for a target!
Like Bunker Hill, two years ago, when I watched all day from the housetop,

Through Father's spy-glass,
The red city, and the blue, bright water,
And puffs of smoke which you made
Twenty miles away,
Round by Cambridge, or over the Neck,
But the smoke was white — white!
To-day the trumpet-flowers are red — red —
And I cannot see you fighting;
But old Mr. Dimond has fled to Canada,
And Myra sings "Yankee Doodle" at her milking.

  The red throats of the trumpets bray and clang in the
      sunshine,
And the smoke-tree puffs dun blossoms into the blue air.

II

The City of Falling Leaves

    Leaves fall,
Brown leaves,
Yellow leaves streaked with brown.
They fall,
Flutter,
Fall again.
The brown leaves,
And the streaked yellow leaves,
Loosen on their branches
And drift slowly downwards.
One,
One, two, three,
One, two, five.

All Venice is a falling of autumn leaves —
Brown,
And yellow streaked with brown.

"That sonnet, Abate,
Beautiful,
I am quite exhausted by it.
Your phrases turn about my heart,
And stifle me to swooning.
Open the window, I beg.
Lord! What a strumming of fiddles and mandolins!
'T is really a shame to stop indoors.
Call my maid, or I will make you lace me yourself.
Fie, how hot it is, not a breath of air!
See how straight the leaves are falling.
Marianna, I will have the yellow satin caught up with
    silver fringe,
It peeps out delightfully from under a mantle.
Am I well painted to-day, *caro Abate mio?*
You will be proud of me at the Ridotto, hey?
Proud of being *cavaliere servente* to such a lady?"
"Can you doubt it, *bellissima Contessa?*
A pinch more rouge on the right cheek,
And Venus herself shines less . . ."
"You bore me, Abate,
I vow I must change you!
A letter, Achmet?
Run and look out of the window, Abate.
I will read my letter in peace."

The little black slave with the yellow satin turban
Gazes at his mistress with strained eyes.

His yellow turban and black skin
Are gorgeous — barbaric.
The yellow satin dress with its silver flashings
Lies on a chair,
Beside a black mantle and a black mask.
Yellow and black,
Gorgeous — barbaric.
The lady reads her letter,
And the leaves drift slowly
Past the long windows.
"How silly you look, my dear Abate,
With that great brown leaf in your wig.
Pluck it off, I beg you,
Or I shall die of laughing."

   A yellow wall,
Aflare in the sunlight,
Chequered with shadows —
Shadows of vine-leaves,
Shadows of masks.
Masks coming, printing themselves for an instant,
Then passing on,
More masks always replacing them.
Masks with tricorns and rapiers sticking out behind
Pursuing masks with veils and high heels,
The sunlight shining under their insteps.
One,
One, two,
One, two, three,
There is a thronging of shadows on the hot wall,
Filigreed at the top with moving leaves.
Yellow sunlight and black shadows,

Yellow and black,
Gorgeous — barbaric.
Two masks stand together,
And the shadow of a leaf falls through them,
Marking the wall where they are not.
From hat-tip to shoulder-tip,
From elbow to sword-hilt,
The leaf falls.
The shadows mingle,
Blur together,
Slide along the wall and disappear.

    Gold of mosaics and candles,
And night-blackness lurking in the ceiling beams.
Saint Mark's glitters with flames and reflections.
A cloak brushes aside,
And the yellow of satin
Licks out over the colored inlays of the pavement.
Under the gold crucifixes
There is a meeting of hands
Reaching from black mantles.
Sighing embraces, bold investigations,
Hide in confessionals,
Sheltered by the shuffling of feet.
Gorgeous — barbaric.
In its mail of jewels and gold,
Saint Mark's looks down at the swarm of black masks;
And outside in the palace gardens brown leaves fall,
Flutter,
Fall.
Brown,
And yellow streaked with brown.

Blue-black the sky over Venice,
With a pricking of yellow stars.
There is no moon,
And the waves push darkly against the prow
Of the gondola,
Coming from Malamocco
And streaming toward Venice.
It is black under the gondola hood,
But the yellow of a satin dress
Glares out like the eye of a watching tiger.
Yellow compassed about with darkness,
Yellow and black,
Gorgeous — barbaric.
The boatman sings,
It is Tasso that he sings;
The lovers seek each other beneath their mantles,
And the gondola drifts over the lagoon, aslant to the coming dawn.
But at Malamocco in front,
In Venice behind,
Fall the leaves,
Brown,
And yellow streaked with brown.
They fall,
Flutter,
Fall.

Poetry: A Magazine of Verse   *Amy Lowell*

78 *Letters from Egypt*

MEMPHIS and Karnak, Luxor, Thebes, the Nile:
   Of these your letters told; and I who read
Saw loom on dim horizons Egypt's dead
In march across the desert, mile on mile,
A ghostly caravan in slow defile
   Between the sand and stars; and at their head
   From unmapped darkness into darkness fled
The gods that Egypt feared a little while.

There black against the night I saw them loom
   With captive kings and armies in array
Remembered only by their sculptured doom,
   And thought: What Egypt was are we to-day.
Then rose obscure against the rearward gloom
   The march of empires yet to pass away.

The Poetry Journal   *Louis V. Ledoux*

79 *In the Roman Forum*

NOTHING but beauty, now.
   No longer at the point of goading fear
The sullen, tributary world comes near
Before all-subjugating Rome to bow.
No more the pavement of the Forum rings
To breathless Victory's exultant tread
Before the heavy march of captive kings.
Here stood the royal dead
In sculptured immortality, their gaze
Remote above the turmoil of the street
Hoarse with its living struggle at their feet.

Here spoke the law — that voice of bronze was heard
By all the world, and stirred
The latent mind of nations in the bud.
Bright with the laurels, bitter with the blood
Of heroes upon heroes was this place
Where the strong heart of an imperial race
Beat with the essence of a nation's life.
Princes and people evermore at strife —
Incense and worship — clash of armored rage —
Ambition soaring up the sky like flame —
Interminable war that mortals wage
From century to century the same.
Still Fortune holds the crown for those who dare;
Mankind in many a distant otherwhere
Leaps panting toward the promise of her face —
But here, no more of coveting nor care.
No longer here the weltering human tide
Sluices the market-place and scatters wide
The weak as foam, to perish where they list.
Now by the Sovereign Silence purified,
Spring showers all with fragrant amethyst.
Were once these pulses violent and swift
As those that shake the cities of to-day?
How indolently sweet the petals drift
From yonder nodding spray!
Warming their broidered raiment in the sun,
The little bright-eyed lizards bask and run
O'er fallen temples gracious in decay.
Man's arrogance with calculated art
Boasted in marble — now the quiet heart
Of the Great Mother dreams eternal things
In brief bright roses and ethereal green,

Or more exuberant, sings
In poppies poured profusely to the air
From secret hoards of scarlet.   Nothing seen
But swoons with beauty — beauty everywhere —
Nothing but beauty . . . now.
Here is the immortality of Rome.
Not where the city rises, dome on dome,
Seek we the living soul of ancient might,
But in this temple of green silence — here
Flame purer than the vestal is alight.
The world again draws near
In reverence, but now it comes to pay
The tribute of a nobler coin than fear.
In wondering worship, not in fierce dismay,
Men bow the knee to what of Rome remains.
Time's long lustration has effaced her stains.
All that is perishable now is past
And earth her portion tenderly transmutes
To evanescent beauty of her own,
Jubilant flowers and nectar-breathing fruits —
Living in deathless glory at the last
Divinity alone.
The Bellman   *Amelia Josephine Burr*

80   *The Sin Eater*

I

HARK ye! Hush ye! Margot's dead!
   Hush! Have done wi' your brawling tune!
Danced, she did, till the stars grew pale;
Mother o' God, an' she's gone at noon!

Sh-h . . . d'ye *hear* me? — Margot's *dead!*
Sickened an' drooped an' died in an hour!
(Bring me th' milk an' th' meat an' bread.)
Drooped, she did, like a wilted flower.
Come an' look at her, how she lies,
Little an' lone, and like she's scared. . . .
(She lost her beads last Friday week,
Tore her Book, an' she never cared.) . . .
Eh, my lass, but it's winter, now —
You that ever was meant for June,
Your laughing mouth an' your dancing feet —
An' now you're done, like an ended tune.
Where's that woman? Ah, give it me quick,
Food at her head an' her poor, still feet. . . .
There's plenty, fool! D'ye think the wench
Had *so* many sins for himself to eat?
Take up your cloak an' hand me mine. . . .
Are we fetchin' him? Eh, for sure!
An' you'll come with me for all your quakes,
Clear to his cave across the moor!
— Margot, dearie, don't look so scared,
It's no long while till your peace begins!
What if you tore your Book, poor lamb?
I'm bringin' you one will eat your sins!

II

It's a blood-red sun that's sinkin'. . . .
Ohooo, but the marshland's drear!
Woman, for why will you be shrinkin'?
I'm tellin' you there's nought to fear.
What if the twilight's gloomish
An' th' shadows creep an' crawl? —

Woman, woman, here'll be th' cave!
Stand by me close till I call!
    "Sin Eater! Devil Cheater!"
    (Eh, it echoes hollowly!)
"Margot's dead at Willow Farm!
Shroud your face and follow me!"

III

One o' th' clock . . . two o' th' clock. . . .
This night's a week in span!
Still he crouches by her side. . . .
Devil . . . ghost . . . or man? . . .

IV

Woman, never cock's crow sounded sweet before!
Set the casement wide ajar, fasten back the door!
Eh, but I be cold an' stiff, waitin' for th' dawn;
Fetch me flowers — jessamine — see, the food is gone. . . .
Light enough to see her now. . . . Mary! How her face
Shines on us like altar fires, now she's sure o' grace!
Never mind your Book, my lamb, never mind your beads,
There's th' Gleam before you now, follow where it leads.

V

Tearful peace and gentle grief
Brood on Willow Farm:
Margot, sleeping in her flowers,
Smiles, secure from harm:
In a cave across the moor,
Dank and dark within,
Moans the trafficker in souls,
Freshly bowed with sin.
  The Smart Set   *Ruth Comfort Mitchell*

81 *Eye-Witness*

DOWN by the railroad in a green valley
   By dancing water, there he stayed awhile
Singing, and three men with him, listeners,
All tramps, all homeless reapers of the wind,
Motionless now and while the song went on
Transfigured into mages thronged with visions;
There with the late light of the sunset on them
And on clear water spinning from a spring
Through little cones of sand dancing and fading,
Close beside pine woods where a hermit-thrush
Cast, when love dazzled him, shadows of music
That lengthened, fluting, through the singer's pauses
While the sure earth rolled eastward bringing stars
Over the singer and the men that listened
There by the roadside, understanding all.

A train went by but nothing seemed to be changed.
Some eye at a car window must have flashed
From the plush world inside the glassy Pullman,
Carelessly bearing off the scene for ever,
With idle wonder what the men were doing,
Seeing they were so strangely fixed and seeing
Torn papers from their smeary dreary meal
Spread on the ground with old tomato cans
Muddy with dregs of lukewarm chicory,
Neglected while they listened to the song.

And while he sang the singer's face was lifted,
And the sky shook down a soft light upon him

Out of its branches where like fruits there were
Many beautiful stars and planets moving,
With lands upon them, rising from their seas,
Glorious lands with glittering sands upon them,
With soils of gold and magic mould for seeding,
The shining loam of lands afoam with gardens
On mightier stars with giant rains and suns
There in the heavens; but on none of all
Was there ground better than he stood upon:
There was no world there in the sky above him
Deeper in promise than the earth beneath him
Whose dust had flowered up in him the singer
And three men understanding every word.

The Tramp Sings:

I will sing, I will go, and never ask me "Why?"
I was born a rover and a passer-by.

I seem to myself like water and sky,
A river and a rover and a passer-by.

But in the winter three years back
We lit us a night fire by the track,

And the snow came up and the fire it flew
And we could n't find the warming room for two.

One had to suffer, so I left him the fire
And I went to the weather from my heart's desire.

It was night on the line, it was no more fire,
But the zero whistle through the icy wire.

As I went suffering through the snow
Something like a shadow came moving slow.

I went up to it and I said a word;
Something flew above it like a kind of bird.

I leaned in closer and I saw a face;
A light went round me but I kept my place.

My heart went open like an apple sliced;
I saw my Saviour and I saw my Christ.

Well, you may not read it in a book,
But it takes a gentle Saviour to give a gentle look.

I looked in his eyes and I read the news;
His heart was having the railroad blues.

Oh, the railroad blues will cost you dear,
Keeps you moving on for something that you don't see
    here.

We stood and whispered in a kind of moon;
The line was looking like May and June.

I found he was a roamer and a journey man,
Looking for a lodging since the night began.

He went to the doors but he did n't have the pay,
He went to the windows, then he went away.

Says: "We'll walk together and we'll both be fed,"
Says: "I will give you the 'other' bread."

OF MAGAZINE VERSE

Oh, the bread he gave and without money!
O drink, O fire, O burning honey!

It went all through me like a shining storm:
I saw inside me, it was light and warm.

I saw deep under and I saw above,
I saw the stars weighed down with love.

They sang that love to burning birth,
They poured that music to the earth.

I heard the stars sing low like mothers.
He said: "Now look, and help feed others."

I looked around, and as close as touch
Was everybody that suffered much.

They reached out, there was darkness only;
They could not see us, they were lonely.

I saw the hearts that deaths took hold of,
With the wounds bare that were not told of;

Hearts with things in them making gashes;
Hearts that were choked with their dreams' ashes;

Women in front of the rolled-back air,
Looking at their breasts and nothing there;

Good men wasting and trapped in hells;
Hurt lads shivering with the fare-thee-wells.

I saw them as if something bound them;
I stood there but my heart went round them.

I begged him not to let me see them wasted.
Says: "Tell them then what you have tasted."

Told him I was weak as a rained-on bee;
Told him I was lost. — Says: "Lean on me."

Something happened then I could not tell,
But I knew I had the water for every hell.

Any other thing it was no use bringing;
They needed what the stars were singing,

What the whole sky sang like waves of light,
The tune that it danced to, day and night.

Oh, I listened to the sky for the tune to come;
The song seemed easy, but I stood there dumb.

The stars could feel me reaching through them;
They let down light and drew me to them.

I stood in the sky in a light like day,
Drinking in the words that all things say

Where the worlds hang growing in clustered shapes
Dripping the music like wine from grapes.

With "Love, Love, Love," above the pain,
— The vine-like song with its wine-like rain.

Through heaven under heaven the song takes root
Of the turning, burning, deathless fruit.

I came to the earth and the pain so near me,
I tried that song but they could n't hear me.

I went down into the ground to grow,
A seed for a song that would make men know.

Into the ground from my Roamer's light
I went; he watched me sink to night.

Deep in the ground from my human grieving,
His pain ploughed in me to believing.

Oh, he took earth's pain to be his bride,
While the heart of life sang in his side.

For I felt that pain, I took its kiss,
My heart broke into dust with his.

Then sudden through the earth I found life springing;
The dust men trampled on was singing.

Deep in my dust I felt its tones;
The roots of beauty went round my bones.

I stirred, I rose like a flame, like a river,
I stood on the line, I could sing for ever.

Love had pierced into my human sheathing,
Song came out of me simple as breathing.

A freight came by, the line grew colder.
He laid his hand upon my shoulder.

Says, "Don't stay on the line such nights,"
And led me by the hand to the station lights.

I asked him in front of the station-house wall
If he had lodging.   Says: "None at all."

I pointed to my heart and looked in his face. —
"Here, — if you have n't got a better place."

He looked and he said: "Oh, we still must roam
But if you'll keep it open, well, I'll call it 'home.'"

The thrush now slept whose pillow was his wing.
So the song ended and the four remained
Still in the faint starshine that silvered them,
While the low sound went on of broken water
Out of the spring and through the darkness flowing
Over a stone that held it from the sea.
Whether the men spoke after could not be told,
A mist from the ground so veiled them, but they waited
A little longer till the moon came up;
Then on the gilded track leading to the mountains,
Against the moon they faded in common gold
And earth bore East with all toward the new morning.
 Scribner's Magazine   *Ridgely Torrence*

82   *The Gift of God*

BLESSED with a joy that only she
Of all alive shall ever know,
She wears a proud humility
For what it was that willed it so, —
That her degree should be so great
Among the favored of the Lord
That she may scarcely bear the weight
Of her bewildering reward.

As one apart, immune, alone,
Or featured for the shining ones,
And like to none that she has known
Of other women's other sons, —
The firm fruition of her need,
He shines anointed; and he blurs
Her vision, till it seems indeed
A sacrilege to call him hers.

She fears a little for so much
Of what is best, and hardly dares
To think of him as one to touch
With aches, indignities, and cares;
She sees him rather at the goal,
Still shining; and her dream foretells
The proper shining of a soul
Where nothing ordinary dwells.

Perchance a canvass of the town
Would find him far from flags and shouts,
And leave him only the renown
Of many smiles and many doubts;

Perchance the crude and common tongue
Would havoc strangely with his worth;
But she, with innocence unwrung,
Would read his name around the earth.

And others, knowing how this youth
Would shine, if love could make him great,
When caught and tortured for the truth
Would only writhe and hesitate;
While she, arranging for his days
What centuries could not fulfil,
Transmutes him with her faith and praise,
And has him shining where she will.

She crowns him with her gratefulness,
And says again that life is good;
And should the gift of God be less
In him than in her motherhood,
His fame, though vague, will not be small,
As upward through her dream he fares,
Half clouded with a crimson fall
Of roses thrown on marble stairs.

Scribner's Magazine   *Edwin Arlington Robinson*

83   *Meanwhile*

THE August sun had still two hours of sky
    When the white flag a-flutter from the house
Signalled him in to find his wife at watch
At the boy's bed. He laid his calloused hand
Lightly on that soft face now fever flushed.
"Much worse," she said.

                    "Yes, much worse. I'll ride Jeff
Cross-country, try to borrow a saddle horse
At Campbell's. If the doctor is at home —
Get there by one, to-night, and home again
In the morning, maybe eight, at most by nine."
His rough lips touched the boy who moaned and stirred.

The sweating plough-horse changed from jolting trot
To clumsy gallop, soon was winded, fell
Back to a walk, gained breath and galloped on.
At Campbell's ranch few words. They learned his need,
Saddled the pony, promised to relay
The doctor's team in the morning. It was ride.
When sunset came the man was galloping
On gentle prairie. Soon he dropped from the ridge,
Picking a way down canyon banks to follow
In the chill dusk of the draw a winding mile;
Then stiff ascent and upland track. The sky
Afar off held its tender sunset hues,
Slow fading. One by one the big white stars
Budded and blossomed. Sometimes prairie owls
Gave chuckling notes and made dim fluttering.
The balm of cooling dews healed all the air,
And ripening grass was fragrant, and late flowers,
While from the wheeling stars a gentle glow
Fell on the prairies like a luminous veil.
The vast plain's prayer was answered utterly.

As the dusk gathered in the little room
The woman still could see the pillow white,
And the child's tousled hair in outline dark
About his face. He broke from out his sleep
Babbling of strange wild fancies; hardly knew

At times, his name, her kindness. Lest the dark
Loose more disorder in his wits, she brought
A lighted lamp and sang old ballad songs
In a soft voice that won him ease again,
And quiet breathings. She could hear the clock
Lag noisily, and from the distant draws
The shrill wail of the coyote, and close by
The creaking misery of some cricket-thing.
Minutes seemed hours. She would try to read.
She got her Bible, but the tears came fast.
Try praying: surely there is help in prayer
That the boy should recover, that her man
Might find the doctor ready. She can see
As in a living vision the sunshine,
The doctor's rattling buggy racing up
In time.

       In time? Thus praying, a slight noise
Led her eyes to the door. She saw it move,
Open, and a strange, dirty face looked in
Bristling with thickets of wild, brush-like beard.
How her heart did beat! She did not rise nor scream,
But with a finger at her lip, said, "Hush.
My boy is sick, out of his head, indeed,
And must not see you. It might make him die.
So leave us. Maybe you are hungry. Look
In the cupboard, you will find some bread and meat,
And coffee on the stove. Go, wash and eat."
Came a low "Thank ye," and the door went shut.
She turned to where the clock hands pointed ten.
There would be minutes while the tramp would eat, —
This outcast fifty miles from the grading camps

Meant anything. She could not think nor move,
A chill so numbed her, weakening every pulse.
But something somehow steadied all her tone
When the door opened once more, and the voice
Asked, "Is there only you?"

                                      "My husband's gone
For the doctor, and should be here even now.
Hush, the boy's waking. Go to the pump, and bring
Cold water for the headcloths. Put the bucket
Upon the table. In the shed you will find
Fresh hay and blankets."

                                     He was gone. Once more
The sweet voice crooning low the ballad tune
Without a tremble or any sign of fear
Mastered the boy's wild fancies, brought him rest.
She listened to the clock, and hours went by;
She looked out to the stars, and hours went by;
At last a grayness, light grew, dawn increased, —
In two more hours. At nine o'clock they came
In time and happily.

                      How like a tale,
Or a heart-breaking dream the afterwards!
But while death's presence from the noiseless dark
Saturates all the air of some child's room
Where the mother prays for one more breath un-
    harmed —
Meanwhile — how measure her agony of fear?
How ease the watching of her wide-stretched eyes?

                                          Edwin Ford Piper
The Midland: A Magazine of the Middle West

84   *Grieve not, Ladies*

OH, grieve not, Ladies, if at night
   Ye wake to feel your beauty going.
It was a web of frail delight,
   Inconstant as an April snowing.

In other eyes, in other lands,
   In deep fair pools, new beauty lingers,
But like spent water in your hands
   It runs from your reluctant fingers.

Ye shall not keep the singing lark
   That owes to earlier skies its duty.
Weep not to hear along the dark
   The sound of your departing beauty.

The fine and anguished ear of night
   Is tuned to hear the smallest sorrow.
Oh, wait until the morning light!
   It may not seem so gone to-morrow!

But honey-pale and rosy-red!
   Brief lights that made a little shining!
Beautiful looks about us shed —
   They leave us to the old repining.

Think not the watchful dim despair
   Has come to you the first, sweet-hearted!
For oh, the gold in Helen's hair!
   And how she cried when that departed!

Perhaps that one that took the most,
  The swiftest borrower, wildest spender,
May count, as we would not, the cost —
  And grow more true to us and tender.

Happy are we if in his eyes
  We see no shadow of forgetting.
Nay — if our star sinks in those skies
  We shall not wholly see its setting.

Then let us laugh as do the brooks
  That such immortal youth is ours,
If memory keeps for them our looks
  As fresh as are the spring-time flowers.

Oh, grieve not, Ladies, if at night
  Ye wake, to feel the cold December!
Rather recall the early light
  And in your loved one's arms, remember.

The Atlantic Monthly   *Anna Hempstead Branch*

85   *Cool Tombs*

WHEN Abraham Lincoln was shoveled into the tombs he forgot the copperheads and the assassin . . . in the dust, in the cool tombs.

And Ulysses Grant lost all thought of con men and Wall Street, cash and collateral turned ashes . . . in the dust, in the cool tombs.

Pocahontas' body, lovely as a poplar, sweet as a red haw in November or a paw-paw in May, did she wonder, does she remember? . . . in the dust, in the cool tombs?

Take any streetful of people buying clothes and groceries, cheering a hero or throwing confetti and blowing tin horns . . . tell me if the lovers are losers . . . tell me if any get more than lovers . . . in the dust . . . in the cool tombs.

The Craftsman   *Carl Sandburg*

86 *Memories of Whitman and Lincoln*

"*When lilacs last in the dooryard bloom'd.*" —W. W.

LILACS shall bloom for Walt Whitman
And lilacs for Abraham Lincoln.
Spring hangs in the dew of the dooryards
These memories — these memories —
They hang in the dew for the bard who fetched
A sprig of them once for his brother
When he lay cold and dead. . . .
And forever now when America leans in the dooryard
And over the hills Spring dances,
Smell of lilacs and sight of lilacs shall bring to her heart
  these brothers. . . .
Lilacs shall bloom for Walt Whitman
And lilacs for Abraham Lincoln.

. . . .

Who are the shadow-forms crowding the the night?
What shadows of men?
The still star-night is high with these brooding spirits —
Their shoulders rise on the Earth-rim, and they are great
  presences in heaven —

They move through the stars like outlined winds in young-leaved maples.
Lilacs bloom for Walt Whitman
And lilacs for Abraham Lincoln.
Deeply the nation throbs with a world's anguish —

But it sleeps, and I on the housetops
Commune with souls long dead who guard our land at midnight,
A strength in each hushed heart —
I seem to hear the Atlantic moaning on our shores with the plaint of the dying
And rolling on our shores with the rumble of battle. . . .
I seem to see my country growing golden toward California,
And, as fields of daisies, a people, with slumbering upturned faces
Leaned over by Two Brothers,
And the greatness that is gone.

. . . .

Lilacs bloom for Walt Whitman
And lilacs for Abraham Lincoln.

. . . .

Spring runs over the land,
A young girl, light-footed, eager . . .
For I hear a song that is faint and sweet with first love,
Out of the West, fresh with the grass and the timber,
But dreamily soothing the sleepers. . . .
I listen: I drink it deep.

. . . .

Softly the Spring sings,
Softly and clearly:

"*I open lilacs for the beloved,*
  Lilacs for the lost, the dead.
And, see, for the living, I bring sweet strawberry blossoms,
And I bring buttercups, and I bring to the woods anemones
    and blue bells . . .
I open lilacs for the beloved,
And when my fluttering garment drifts through dusty cities,
And blows on hills, and brushes the inland sea,
Over you, sleepers, over you, tired sleepers,
A fragrant memory falls . . .
I open love in the shut heart,
I open lilacs for the beloved."

 . . . .

Lilacs bloom for Walt Whitman
And lilacs for Abraham Lincoln.

 . . . .

Was that the Spring that sang, opening locked hearts,
And is remembrance mine?
For I know these two great shadows in the spacious night,
Shadows folding America close between them,
Close to the heart . . .
And I know how my own lost youth grew up blessedly in
    their spirit,
And how the morning song of the mighty native bard
Sent me out from my dreams to the living America,
To the chanting seas, to the piney hills, down the railroad
    vistas,
Out into the streets of Manhattan when the whistles blew
    at seven,
Down to the mills of Pittsburgh and the rude faces of
    labor . . .

And I know how the grave great music of that other,
Music in which lost armies sang requiems,
And the vision of that gaunt, that great and solemn figure,
And the graven face, the deep eyes, the mouth,
O human-hearted brother,
Dedicated anew my undevoted heart
To America, my land.

. . . .

Lilacs bloom for Walt Whitman
And lilacs for Abraham Lincoln.

. . . .

Now in this hour I was suppliant to these two brothers,
And I said: Your land has need:
Half-awakened and blindly we grope in the great
  world. . . .
What strength may we take from our Past, what promise
  hold for our Future?

And the one brother leaned and whispered:
"I put my strength in a book,
And in that book my love. . . .
This, with my love, I give to America. . . ."
And the other brother leaned and murmured:
"I put my strength in a life,
And in that life my love,
This, with my love, I give to America."

. . . .

Lilacs bloom for Walt Whitman
And lilacs for Abraham Lincoln.

. . . .

Then my heart sang out: This strength shall be our
    strength:
Yea, when the great hour comes, and the sleepers wake
    and are hurled back,
And creep down into themselves
There shall they find Walt Whitman
And there, Abraham Lincoln.

   .   .   .   .

O Spring, go over this land with much singing
And open the lilacs everywhere,
Open them out with the old-time fragrance
Making a people remember that something has been
    forgotten,
Something is hidden deep — strange memories — strange
    memories —
Of him that brought a sprig of the purple cluster
To him that was mourned of all. . . .
And so they are linked together
While yet America lives. . . .

   .   .   .   .

While yet America lives, my heart,
Lilacs shall bloom for Walt Whitman
And lilacs for Abraham Lincoln.
  The Seven Arts   *James Oppenheim*

87   *Autochthon*

IN a rude country some four thousand miles
   From Charles' and Alfred's birthplace you were born,
In the same year. But Charles and you were born
On the same day, and Alfred six months later.

Thus start you in a sense the race together. . . . .
Charles goes to Edinburgh, afterwards
His father picks him for the ministry,
And sends him off to Cambridge where he spends
His time on beetles and geology,
Neglects theology. Alfred is here
Fondling a Virgil and a Horace.
But you — these years you give to reading Æsop,
The Bible, lives of Washington and Franklin,
And Kirkham's grammar.

In 1830 Alfred prints a book
Containing "Mariana," certain other
Delicate, wind-blown bells of airy music.
And in this year you move from Indiana
And settle near Decatur, Illinois,
Hard by the river Sangamon where fever
And ague burned and shook the poor
Swamp saffron creatures of that desolate land.
While Alfred walks the flowering lanes of England,
And reads Theocritus to the song of larks
You clear the forests, plow the stumpy land,
Fight off the torments of mosquitoes, flies
And study Kirkham's grammar.

In 1831 Charles takes a trip
Around the world, sees South America,
And studies living things in Galapagos,
Tahiti, Keeling Island and Tasmania.
In 1831 you take a trip
Upon a flat-boat down to New Orleans

Through hardships scarcely less than Joliet
And Marquette knew in 1673,
Return on foot to Orfutt's store at Salem.

By this time Jacques Rousseau was canonized;
Jefferson dead but seven years or so;
Brook Farm was budding, Garrison had started
His *Liberator*, Fourier still alive;
And Emerson was preening his slim wings
For flights into broad spaces — there was stir
Enough to sweep the Shelleyan heads, — in truth
Shelley was scarcely passed a decade then.
Old Goodwin still was writing, wars for freedom
Swept through the Grecian Isles, America
Had "isms" in abundance, but not one
Took hold of you.

In 1832 Alfred has drawn
Out of old Mallory and Grecian myths
The "Lady of Shalott" and fair "Œnone,"
And put them into verse.
This is the year you fight the Black Hawk war,
And issue an address to Sangamon's people.
You are but twenty-three, yet this address
Would not shame Charles or Alfred; it's restrained,
And sanely balanced, without extra words,
Or youth's conceits, or imitative figures, dreams
Or "isms" of the day. No, here you hope
That enterprise, morality, sobriety
May be more general, and speak a word
For popular education, so that all
May have a "moderate education" as you say.

OF MAGAZINE VERSE

You make a plea for railroads and canals,
And ask the suffrages of the people, saying
You have known disappointment far too much
To be chagrined at failure, if you lose.
They take you at your word and send another
To represent them in the Legislature.
Then you decide to learn the blacksmith's trade.
But Fate comes by and plucks you by the sleeve,
And changes history, doubtless.

By '36 when Charles returns to England
You have become a legislator; yes
You tried again and won. You have become
A lawyer too, by working through the levels
Of laborer, store-keeper and surveyor,
Wrapped up in problems of geometry,
And Kirkham's grammar and Sir William Blackstone,
And Coke on Littleton, and Joseph Chitty.
Brook Farm will soon bloom forth, François Fourier
Is still on earth, and Garrison is shaking
Terrible lightning at Slavocracy.
And certain libertarians, *videlicet*
John Greenleaf Whittier and others, sing
The trampling out of grapes of wrath; in truth
The Hebrews taught the idealist how to sing
Destruction in the name of God and curse
Where strength was lacking for the sword — but you
Are not a Robert Emmet, or a Shelley,
Have no false dreams of dying to bring in
The day of Liberty. At twenty-three
You're measuring the world and waiting for
Dawn's mists to clear that you may measure it,

And know the field's dimensions ere you put
Your handle to the plow.

In 1833 a man named Hallam,
A friend of Alfred's died at twenty-two.
Thereafter Alfred worked his hopes and fears
Upon the dark impasto of this loss
In delicate colors.   And in 1850
When you were sunk in melancholia,
As one of no use in the world, adjudged
To be of no use by your time and place,
Alfred brought forth his Dante dream of life,
Received the laureate wreath and settled down
With a fair wife amid entrancing richness
Of sunny seas and silken sails and dreams
Of Araby,
And ivied halls, and meadows where the breeze
Of temperate England blows the hurrying cloud.
There, seated like an Oriental king
In silk and linen clothed took the acclaim
Of England and the world! . . .
                              This is the year
You sit in a little office there in Springfield,
Feet on the desk and brood.   What are you thinking?
You're forty-one; around you spears are whacking
The wind-mills of the day, you watch and weigh.
The sun-light of your mind quivers about
The darkness every thinking soul must know,
And lights up hidden things behind the door,
And in dark corners.   You have fathomed much,
Weighed life and men.   O what a spheréd brain,
Strong nerved, fresh blooded, firm in plasmic fire,

And ready for a task, if there be one!
That is the question that makes brooding thought:
For you know well men come into the world
And find no task, and die, and are not known —
Great spheréd brains gone into dust again,
Their light under a bushel all their days!
In 1859, Charles publishes
His "Origin of Species," and 't is said
You see it, or at least hear what it is.
Out of three travelers in a distant land
One writes a book of what the three have seen.
Perhaps you never read much, yet perhaps
Some books were just a record of your mind.
How had it helped you in your work to read
The "Idylls of the King"? As much, perhaps,
Had Alfred read the Northwest Ordinance
Of 1787. . . .

               But in this year
Of '59 you're sunk in blackest thought
About the country maybe, but, I think,
About this riddle of our mortal life.
You were a poet, Abraham, from your birth.
That makes you think, and makes you deal at last
With things material to the tune of laws
Moving in higher spaces when you're called
To act — and show a poet moulding stuff
Too tough for spirits practical to mould.
Here are you with your feet upon the desk.
You have been beaten in a cause which kept
Some strings too loose to catch the vibrate waves
Of a great Harp whose music you have sensed.

You are a mathematician using symbols
Like Justice, Truth, with keenness to perceive
Disturbance of equations, a logician
Who sees invariable laws, and beauty born
Of finding out and following the laws.
You are a Plato brooding there in Springfield.
You are a poet with a voice for Truth,
And never to be claimed by visionaries
Who chant the theme of bread and bread alone.

                                            But here and now
They want you not for Senator, it seems.
You have been tossed to one side by the rush
Of world events, left stranded and alone,
And fitted for no use, it seems, in Springfield.
A country lawyer with a solid logic,
And gift of prudent phrase which has a way
Of hardening under time to rock as hard
As the enduring thought you seal it with.
You've reached your fiftieth year, your occultation
Should pass. If ever, we should see a light:
In all your life you have not seen a city.
But now our Springfield giant strides Broadway,
Thrills William Cullen Bryant, sets a wonder
Going about the East, that Kirkham's grammar
Can give a man such speech at Cooper Union,
Which even Alfred's, trained to Virgil's style,
Cannot disdain for matching in the thought
With faultless clearness.

And still in 1860 all the Brahmins
Have fear to give you power.
You are a backwoodsman, a country lawyer

Unlettered in the difficult art of states.
A denizen of a squalid western town,
Dowered with a knack of argument alone,
Which wakes the country school-house, and may lift
Its devotees to Congress by good fortune.
But then at Cooper Union intuitive eyes
Had measured your tall frame, and careful speech,
Your strength and self-possession.   Then they came
With that dramatic sense which is American
Into the hall with rails which you had split,
And called you Honest Abe, and wearing badges
With your face on them and the poor catch words
Of Honest Abe, as if you were a referee
Like Honest Kelly, when in truth no man
Had ever been your intimate, ever slapped you
With brisk familiarity, or called you
Anything but Mr. Lincoln, never
Abe, or Abraham, and never used
The Hello Bill of salutation to you —
O great patrician, therefore fit to be
Great democrat as well!

In 1862 Charles publishes
"How Orchid Flowers are Fertilized by Insects,"
And you give forth a proclamation saying
"The Union must have peace, or I wipe out
The blot of Negro slavery.   You see,
The symphony's the thing, and if you mar it,
Contending over slavery, I remove
The source of the disharmony.   I admit
The freedom of the press — but for the Union.
When you abuse the Union, you shall stop.

And when you are in jail, no habeas corpus
Shall bring relief — I have suspended it."
To-day they call you libertarian —
Well, so you were, but just as Beauty is,
And Truth is, even if they curb and vanquish
The lower heights of beauty and of truth.
They take your speech and deeds and give you place
In Hebrew temples with Ezekiel,
Habakkuk and Isaiah — you emerge
From this association, master man!
You are not of the faith that breeds the ethic
Wranglers, who make economic goals
The strain and test of life. You are not one,
Spite of your lash and sword threat, who believe
God will avenge the weak. That is the dream
Which builds millenniums where disharmonies
That make the larger harmony shall cease —
A dream not yours. And they shall lose you who
Enthrone you as a prophet who cut through
The circle of our human sphere of life
To let in wrath and judgments, final tests
On Life around the price of sparrows, weights
Wherewith bread shall be weighed. . . .

There is a windless flame where cries and tears,
Where hunger, strife, and war and human blood
No shadow cast, and where the love of Truth,
Which is not love of individual souls,
Finds solace in a Judgment of our life.
That is the Flame that took both Charles and You —
O leader in a Commonwealth of Thought!

Reedy's Mirror   *Edgar Lee Masters*

88   *Lincoln*

I

LIKE a gaunt, scraggly pine
  Which lifts its head above the mournful sandhills;
And patiently, through dull years of bitter silence,
Untended and uncared for, starts to grow.

Ungainly, labouring, huge,
The wind of the north has twisted and gnarled its branches;
Yet in the heat of midsummer days, when thunder-clouds
    ring the horizon,
A nation of men shall rest beneath its shade.

And it shall protect them all,
Hold everyone safe there, watching aloof in silence;
Until at last one mad stray bolt from the zenith
Shall strike it in an instant down to earth.

II

There was a darkness in this man; an immense and hollow
    darkness,
Of which we may not speak, nor share with him, nor enter;
A darkness through which strong roots stretched down-
    wards into the earth
Towards old things;

Towards the herdman-kings who walked the earth and
    spoke with God,
Towards the wanderers who sought for they knew not
    what, and found their goal at last;

Towards the men who waited, only waited patiently
    when all seemed lost,
Many bitter winters of defeat;

Down to the granite of patience
These roots swept, knotted fibrous roots, prying, piercing,
    seeking,
And drew from the living rock and the living waters
    about it·
The red sap to carry upwards to the sun.

Not proud, but humble,
Only to serve and pass on, to endure to the end through
    service;
For the axe is laid at the roots of the trees, and all that
    bring not forth good fruit
Shall be cut down on the day to come and cast into the fire.

III

There is a silence abroad in the land to-day,
And in the hearts of men, a deep and anxious silence;
And, because we are still at last, those bronze lips slowly
    open,
Those hollow and weary eyes take on a gleam of light.

Slowly a patient, firm-syllabled voice cuts through the
    endless silence
Like labouring oxen that drag a plow through the chaos
    of rude clay-fields;
"I went forward as the light goes forward in early spring,
But there were also many things which I left behind.

"Tombs that were quiet;
One, of a mother, whose brief light went out in the darkness,
One, of a loved one, the snow on whose grave is long falling,
One, only of a child, but it was mine.

"Have you forgot your graves? Go, question them in anguish,
Listen long to their unstirred lips. From your hostages to silence,
Learn there is no life without death, no dawn without sunsetting,
No victory but to him who has given all."

IV

The clamour of cannon dies down, the furnace-mouth of the battle is silent.
The midwinter sun dips and descends, the earth takes on afresh its bright colours,
But he whom we mocked and obeyed not, he whom we scorned and mistrusted,
He has descended, like a god, to his rest.

Over the uproar of cities,
Over the million intricate threads of life wavering and crossing,
In the midst of problems we know not, tangling, perplexing, ensnaring,
Rises one white tomb alone.

Beam over it, stars,
Wrap it round, stripes — stripes red for the pain that he bore for you —

Enfold it forever, O flag, rent, soiled, but repaired through
    your anguish;
Long as you keep him there safe, the nations shall bow
    to your law.

Strew over him flowers:
Blue forget-me-nots from the north, and the bright pink
    arbutus
From the east, and from the west rich orange blossom,
But from the heart of the land take the passion-flower;

Rayed, violet, dim,
With the nails that pierced, the cross that he bore and
    the circlet,
And beside it there lay also one lonely snow-white magnolia,
Bitter for remembrance of the healing which has passed.
    The Poetry Review of America   *John Gould Fletcher*

89   *General William Booth Enters into Heaven*

[To be sung to the tune of *The Blood of the Lamb* with indicated instrument]

I

[*Bass drum beaten loudly*]

BOOTH led boldly with his big bass drum —
    (Are you washed in the blood of the Lamb?)
The Saints smiled gravely and they said: "He's come."
(Are you washed in the blood of the Lamb?)
Walking lepers followed, rank on rank,
Lurching bravoes from the ditches dank,

Drabs from the alleyways and drug fiends pale —
Minds still passion-ridden, soul-powers frail: —
Vermin-eaten saints with mouldy breath,
Unwashed legions with the ways of Death —
(Are you washed in the blood of the Lamb?)

   [*Banjos*]
Every slum had sent its half-a-score
The round world over. (Booth had groaned for more.)
Every banner that the wide world flies
Bloomed with glory and transcendent dyes.
Big-voiced lasses made their banjos bang,
Tranced, fanatical they shrieked and sang: —
"Are you washed in the blood of the Lamb?"
Hallelujah! It was queer to see
Bull-necked convicts with that land make free.
Loons with trumpets blowed a blare, blare, blare
On, on upward thro' the golden air!
(Are you washed in the blood of the Lamb?)

II

   [*Bass drum slower and softer*]
Booth died blind and still by Faith he trod,
Eyes still dazzled by the ways of God.
Booth led boldly, and he looked the chief
Eagle countenance in sharp relief,
Beard a-flying, air of high command
Unabated in that holy land.

   [*Sweet flute music*]
Jesus came from out the court-house door,
Stretched his hands above the passing poor.

Booth saw not, but led his queer ones there
Round and round the mighty court-house square.
Yet in an instant all that blear review
Marched on spotless, clad in raiment new.
The lame were straightened, withered limbs uncurled
And blind eyes opened on a new, sweet world.

[Bass drum louder]
Drabs and vixens in a flash made whole!
Gone was the weasel-head, the snout, the jowl!
Sages and sibyls now, and athletes clean,
Rulers of empires, and of forests green!

[Grand chorus of all instruments. Tambourines to the foreground]
The hosts were sandalled, and their wings were fire!
(Are you washed in the blood of the Lamb?)
But their noise played havoc with the angel-choir.
(Are you washed in the blood of the Lamb?)
O, shout Salvation! It was good to see
Kings and Princes by the Lamb set free.
The banjos rattled and the tambourines
Jing-jing-jingled in the hands of Queens.

[Reverently sung, no instruments]
And when Booth halted by the curb for prayer
He saw his Master thro' the flag-filled air.
Christ came gently with a robe and crown
For Booth the soldier, while the throng knelt down.
He saw King Jesus. They were face to face,
And he knelt a-weeping in that holy place.
Are you washed in the blood of the Lamb?

Poetry: A Magazine of Verse   Vachel Lindsay

The Poppies

THIS is the garden of our joyous care,
 Where such a little time before you died
You walked with pleasant pride
And pointed out your favorites, the rare
Tree roses, and the riotous delight
Of poppies, from the crimson to the white
Sounding the gamut of ecstatic hue.
So richly coloured was all life to you!
You never called the world a vale of tears.
Such long and loving labor overgrown!
How soon the wild undoes your patient years . . .
Not wholly; with each summer's weeds I see
Poppies arise, self-sown.
They are your garden's immortality.

What would be Heaven for you?   It comforts me
To picture you with leisure and with strength
To bring to life at length
Your dreams of beauty — all your soul set free
From the mean goading of necessity,
And from the bodily pain
You bore so bravely, like a galling chain
That heavy grew and heavier each day.
When death struck these away
I knew the magnitude of your release
By your high look of peace.
God knows I had no lack of tears, but they
Were not for you.   My sorrow was my own.
I read — "*I will not leave you comfortless,
But I will come to you.*"   I had not known

The meaning of those words until your death.
You were less near to me when I could press
Your hand and feel your breath
Upon my cheek, than now. You seem so near,
So full of life, so constantly more dear,
I feel it only needs to turn my gaze
To see you standing here
Among your flowers, as in other days.
Like little shouts of exultation sweet
The poppies at my feet
Loose to the wind their petals. Let them die —
From them shall spring new beauty, by and by.
They are not over-greedy for a pledge
Of immortality; they give their best
To earth — God knows the rest.
So did you tread your path across the edge
Of this our visible world. You did not hoard
Your spirit's treasure for a world unseen
Nor chaffer with your God for a reward
Ere you would serve. You did not even trust
Your Master would be just.
You went your way generous and serene,
And gave unquestioning all you had to spend
As friend to friend.
If you had known that all should end in dust
You would have thought it shame to drop your sword,
Because you fought your beasts at Ephesus
Not for yourself — for us,
Who loved in you the love of righteousness.
There is no soul that touched you in the stress
Of that great battle where you did your part
So gallantly, which you did not impress

With your own chivalry.   In every heart
That knew you, there is sown
Some ruddy-blossomed seedling of your own.
Whatever Heaven there beyond may be,
This I can see!

If this dear presence by my love discerned
Be your own self, the self I knew, returned
From larger life in some transfigured guise
Unseen by mortal eyes,
Or if it be your spirit as it grew
Unconsciously of my own self a part,
Could it be any nearer, if I knew,
Or dearer to my heart?
You are in God, as you have always been.
Although I find it sweet
To dream that I shall know you when we meet
In such a garden as you cherished here,
I will not wait until I die, my Dear,
For Heaven to begin.
Sweeter it is to know that I can give
Your deathless bounty to a world in need.
I sow you as the poppy sows her seed,
And in my love you live.
 The Bellman   *Amelia Josephine Burr*

91   *Yellow Clover*

MUST I, who walk alone,
 Come on it still,
This Puck of plants
The wise would do away with,

The sunshine slants
To play with,
Our wee, gold-dusty flower, the yellow clover,
Which once in parting for a time
That then seemed long,
Ere time for you was over,
We sealed our own?
Do you remember yet,
O Soul beyond the stars,
Beyond the uttermost dim bars
Of space,
Dear Soul, who found earth sweet,
Remember by love's grace,
In dreamy hushes of the heavenly song,
How suddenly we halted in our climb,
Lingering, reluctant, up that farthest hill,
Stooped for the blossoms closest to our feet,
And gave them as a token
Each to each,
In lieu of speech,
In lieu of words too grievous to be spoken,
Those little, gypsy, wondering blossoms wet
With a strange dew of tears?

So it began,
This vagabond, unvalued yellow clover,
To be our tenderest language. All the years
It lent a new zest to the summer hours,
As each of us went scheming to surprise
The other with our homely, laureate flowers,
Sonnets and odes
Fringing our daily roads.

Can amaranth and asphodel
Bring merrier laughter to your eyes?
Oh, if the Blest, in their serene abodes,
Keep any wistful consciousness of earth,
Not grandeurs, but the childish ways of love,
Simplicities of mirth,
Must follow them above
With touches of vague homesickness that pass
Like shadows of swift birds across the grass.
Beneath some foreign arch of sky,
How many a time the rover
You or I,
For life oft sundered look from look,
And voice from voice, the transient dearth
Schooling my soul to brook
This distance that no messages may span,
Would chance
Upon our wilding by a lonely well,
Or drowsy watermill,
Or swaying to the chime of convent bell,
Or where the nightingales of old romance
With tragical contraltos fill
Dim solitudes of infinite desire;
And once I joyed to meet
Our peasant gadabout
A trespasser on trim, seigniorial seat,
Twinkling a saucy eye
As potentates paced by.

Our golden cord! our soft, pursuing flame
From friendship's altar fire!
How proudly we would pluck and tame

The dimpling clusters, mutinously gay!
How swiftly they were sent
Far, far away
On journeys wide,
By sea and continent,
Green miles and blue leagues over,
From each of us to each,
That so our hearts might reach,
And touch within the yellow clover,
Love's letter to be glad about
Like sunshine when it came!

My sorrow asks no healing; it is love;
Let love then make me brave
To bear the keen hurts of
This careless summertide,
Ay, of our own poor flower,
Changed with our fatal hour,
For all its sunshine vanished when you died;
Only white clover blossoms on your grave.
The Poetry Review of America   Katharine Lee Bates

92   *Over Night, a Rose*

THAT over night a rose could come
   I, one time did believe,
For when the fairies live with one,
   They wilfully deceive.
But now I know this perfect thing
   Under the frozen sod

In cold and storm grew patiently
    Obedient to God.
My wonder grows, since knowledge came
    Old fancies to dismiss;
And courage comes. Was not the rose
    A winter doing this?
Nor did it know, the weary while,
    What color and perfume
With this completed loveliness
    Lay in that earthly tomb.
So maybe I, who cannot see
    What God wills not to show,
May, some day, bear a rose for Him
    It took my life to grow.
The Boston Transcript   *Caroline Giltinan*

93   *Evensong*

BEAUTY calls and gives no warning,
  Shadows rise and wander on the day.
In the twilight, in the quiet evening,
We shall rise and smile and go away.
Over the flaming leaves
Freezes the sky.
It is the season grieves,
Not you, not I.
All our spring-times, all our summers,
We have kept the longing warm within.
Now we leave the after-comers
To attain the dreams we did not win.

O we have wakened, Sweet, and had our birth,
  And that's the end of earth;
And we have toiled and smiled and kept the light,
  And that's the end of night.
The Atlantic Monthly   *Ridgely Torrence*

94   *Battle Sleep*

SOMEWHERE, O sun, some corner there must be
  Thou visitest, where down the strand
Quietly, still, the waves go out to sea
  From the green fringes of a pastoral land.

Deep in the orchard-bloom the roof-trees stand,
  The brown sheep graze along the bay,
And through the apple-boughs above the sand
  The bees' hum sounds no fainter than the spray.

There through uncounted hours declines the day
  To the low arch of twilight's close,
And, just as night about the moon grows gray,
  One sail leans westward to the fading rose.

Giver of dreams, O thou with scatheless wing
  Forever moving through the fiery hail,
To flame-seared lids the cooling vision bring,
  And let some soul go seaward with that sail!
The Century Magazine   *Edith Wharton*

95   *Song*
From " Flesh: A Gregorian Ode "

EBB on with me across the sunset tide
   And float beyond the waters of the world,
The light of evening slipping from thy side,
   Thy softened voice in waves of silence furled.

Flow on into the flaming morning wine,
   Drowning the land in color. Then on high
Rise in thy candid innocence and shine
   Like to a poplar straight against the sky.
The Boston Transcript   Edward J. O'Brien

96   *A Statue in a Garden*

I WAS a goddess ere the marble found me.
   Wind, wind, delay not!
Waft my spirit where the laurel crowned me!
   Will the wind stay not?

Then tarry, tarry, listen, little swallow!
   An old glory feeds me:
I lay upon the bosom of Apollo!
   Not a bird heeds me.

For here the days are alien. O, to waken
   Mine, mine, with calling!
But on my shoulders bare, like hopes forsaken,
   The dead leaves are falling.

The sky is gray and full of unshed weeping
    As dim down the garden
I wait and watch the early autumn sweeping.
    The stalks fade and harden.

The souls of all the flowers afar have rallied.
    The trees, gaunt, appalling,
Attest the gloom, and on my shoulders pallid
    The dead leaves are falling.

Poetry: A Magazine of Verse   *Agnes Lee*

97   *The Lesser Children*

A THRENODY AT THE HUNTING SEASON

IN the middle of August when the southwest wind
  Blows after sunset through the leisuring air,
And on the sky nightly the mythic Bee
Leads down the sullen dog star to his lair,
After the feverous vigil of July,
When the loud pageant of the year's high noon
Passed up the ways of time to sing and part,
Grief also wandered by
From out the lovers and the leaves of June,
And one night, at the hiding of the moon,
I knew his heart was very Love's own heart.
Deep within dreams he led me out of doors
As from the upper vault the night outpours,
And when I saw that to him all the skies
Yearned as a sea asleep yearns to its shores
He took a little clay and touched my eyes.

What saw I then, what heard?
Multitudes, multitudes, under the moon they stirred!
The weaker brothers of our earthly breed;
Watchmen of whom our safety takes no heed;
Swift helpers of the wind that sowed the seed
Before the first field was or any fruit;
Warriors against the bivouac of the weed;
Earth's earliest ploughmen for the tender root,
All came about my head and at my feet
A thousand, thousand sweet,
With starry eyes not even raised to plead;
Bewildered, driven, hiding, fluttering, mute!
And I beheld and saw them one by one
Pass and become as nothing in the night.
Clothed on with red they were who once were white;
Drooping, who once led armies to the sun,
Of whom the lowly grass now topped the flight:
In scarlet faint, who once were brave in brown;
Climbers and builders of the silent town,
Creepers and burrowers all in crimson dye,
Winged mysteries of song that from the sky
Once dashed long music down.

O who would take away music from the earth?
Have we so much?   Or love upon the hearth?
No more — they faded;
The great trees bending between birth and birth
Sighed for them, and the night wind's hoarse rebuff
Shouted the shame of which I was persuaded.
Shall Nature's only pausing be by men invaded?
Or shall we lay grief's fagots on her shoulders bare?
Has she not borne enough?

Soon will the mirroring woodland pools begin to con her,
And her sad immemorial passion come upon her;
Lo, would you add despair unto despair?
Shall not the Spring be answer to her prayer?
Must her uncomforted heavens overhead,
Weeping, look down on tears and still behold
Only wings broken or a fledgling dead,
Or underfoot the meadows that wore gold
Die, and the leaves go mourning to the mould
Beneath poor dead and desperate feet
Of folk who in next summer's meadows shall not meet?

Who has not seen in the high gulf of light
What, lower, was a bird, but now
Is moored and altered quite
Into an island of unshaded joy?
To whom the mate below upon the bough
Shouts once and brings him from his high employ.
Yet speeding he forgot not of the cloud
Where he from glory sprang and burned aloud,
But took a little of the day,
A little of the colored sky,
And of the joy that would not stay
He wove a song that cannot die.
Then, then — the unfathomable shame;
The one last wrong arose from out the flame,
The ravening hate that hated not was hurled
Bidding the radiant love once more beware,
Bringing one more loneliness on the world,
And one more blindness in the unseen air.
Nor may the smooth regret, the pitying oath
Shed on such utter bitter any leaven.

OF MAGAZINE VERSE

Only the pleading flowers that knew them both
Hold all their bloody petals up to heaven.

Winds of the fall that all year to and fro
Somewhere upon the earth go wandering,
You saw, you moaned, you know:
Withhold not then unto all time to tell
Lest unborn others of us see this thing.
Bring our sleek, comfortable reason low:
Recount how souls grown tremulous as a bell
Came forth each other and the day to greet
In morning air all Indian-Summer sweet,
And crept upstream, through wood or field or brake,
Most tremblingly to take
What crumbs that from the Master's table fell.
Cry with what thronging thunders they were met,
And hide not how the least leaf was made wet.
Cry till no watcher says that all is well
With raucous discord through the leaning spheres.
But tell
With tears, with tears
How the last man is harmed even as they
Who on these dawns are fire, at dusk are clay.
Record the dumb and wise,
No less than those who lived in singing guise,
Whose choric hearts lit each wild green arcade.
Make men to see their eyes,
Forced to suspect behind each reed or rose
The thorn of lurking foes.
And O, before the daylight goes,
After the deed against the skies,
After the last belief and longing dies,

Make men again to see their eyes
Whose piteous casements now all unafraid
Peer out to that far verge where evermore,
Beyond all woe for which a tear atones,
The likeness of our own dishonor moans,
A sea that has no bottom and no shore.

What shall be done
By you, shy folk who cease thus heart by heart?
You for whose fate such fate forever hovers?
O little lovers,
If you would still have nests beneath the sun
Gather your broods about you and depart,
Before the stony forward-pressing faces
Into the lands bereft of any sound;
The solemn and compassionate desert places.
Give unto men no more the strong delight
To know that underneath the frozen ground
Dwells the warm life and all the quick, pure lore.
Take from our eyes the glory of great flight.
Let us behold no more
People untroubled by a Fate's veiled eyes,
Leave us upon an earth of faith forlorn.
No more wild tidings from the sweet far skies
Of love's long utmost heavenward endeavor.
So shall the silence pour on us forever
The streaming arrows of unutterable scorn.

Nor shall the cry of famine be a shield
The altar of a brutish mood to hide.
Stains, stains, upon the lintels of our doors
Wail to be justified.

Shall there be mutterings at the seasons' yield?
Has eye of man seen bared the granary floors?
Are the fields wasted?   Spilled the oil and wine?
Is the fat seed under the clod decayed?
Does ever the fig tree languish or the vine?
Who has beheld the harvest promise fade?
Or any orchard heavy with fruit asway
Withered away?
No, not these things, but grosser things than those
Are the dim parents of a guilt not dim;
Ancestral urges out of old caves blowing,
When Fear watched at our coming and our going
The horror of the chattering face of Whim.
Hates, cruelties new fallen from the trees
Whereto we clung with impulse sad for love,
Shames we have had all time to rid us of,
Disgraces cold and sorrows long bewept,
Recalled, revived, and kept,
Unmeaning quarrels, blood-compelling lust,
And snarling woes from our old home, the dust.

Yet even of these one saving shape may rise;
Fear may unveil our eyes.
For know you not what curse of blight would fall
Upon a land lorn of the sweet sky races
Who day and night keep ward and seneschal
Upon the treasury of the planted spaces?
Then would the locust have his fill,
And the blind worm lay tithe,
The unfed stones rot in the listless mill,
The sound of grinding cease.
No yearning gold would whisper to the scythe,

Hunger at last would prove us of one blood,
The shores of dreams be drowned in tides of need,
Horribly would the whole earth be at peace.
The burden of the grasshopper indeed
Weigh down the green corn and the tender bud,
The plague of Egypt fall upon the wheat,
And the shrill nit would batten in the heat.

But you, O poor of deeds and rich of breath,
Whose eyes have made our eyes a hue abhorred,
Red, eager aids of aid-unneeding Death,
Hunters before the Lord,
If on the flinted marge about your souls
In vain the heaving tide of mourning rolls,
If from your trails unto the crimson goals
The weeper and the weeping must depart,
If lust of blood come on you like a fiery dart
And darken all the dark autumnal air,
Then, then — be fair.
Pluck a young ash tree or a sapling yew
And at the root end fix an iron thorn,
Then forth with rocking laughter of the horn
And passing, with no belling retinue,
All timorous, lesser sippers of the dew,
Seek out some burly guardian of the hills
And set your urgent thew against his thew.
Then shall the hidden wisdoms and the wills
Strive, and bear witness to the trees and clods
How one has dumb lore of the rocks and swales
And one has reason like unto the gods.
Then shall the lagging righteousness ensue,
The powers at last be equal in the scales,

And the man's club and the beast's claw be flails
To winnow the unworthy of the two.
Then on the earth, in the sky and the heavenly court
That broods behind it,
Justice shall be awakened and aware,
Then those who go forth greatly, seeking sport,
Shall doubtless find it,
And all things be fair.
    The Atlantic Monthly   *Ridgely Torrence*

98   *A Thrush in the Moonlight*

IN came the moon and covered me with wonder,
    Touched me and was near me, and made me very still.
In came a rush of song, like rain after thunder,
Pouring importunate on my window-sill.

I lowered my head, I hid it, I would not see nor hear,
The bird song had stricken me, had brought the moon
    too near.
But when I dared to lift my head, night began to fill
With singing in the darkness. And then the thrush grew
    still.

And the moon came in, and silence, on my window-sill.
    Poetry: A Magazine of Verse   *Witter Bynner*

99   *November*

HARK you such sound as quivers? Kings will hear,
    As kings have heard, and tremble on their thrones;
The old will feel the weight of mossy stones;
The young alone will laugh and scoff at fear.

It is the tread of armies marching near,
  From scarlet lands to lands forever pale;
  It is a bugle dying down the gale;
  It is the sudden gushing of a tear.
And it is hands that grope at ghostly doors;
  And romp of spirit-children on the pave;
  It is the tender sighing of the brave
Who fell, ah! long ago, in futile wars;
  It is such sound as death; and, after all,
  'T is but the forest letting dead leaves fall.
  The Bellman   *Mahlon Leonard Fisher*

100   *The Winter Scene*

I

THE rutted roads are all like iron; skies
  Are keen and brilliant; only the oak-leaves cling
In the bare woods, or hardy bitter-sweet;
Drivers have put their sheepskin jackets on;
And all the ponds are sealed with sheeted ice
That rings with stroke of skate and hockey-stick,
Or in the twilight cracks with running whoop.
Bring in the logs of oak and hickory,
And make an ample blaze on the wide hearth.
Now is the time, with winter o'er the world,
For books and friends and yellow candle-light,
And timeless lingering by the settling fire,
While all the shuddering stars are keen and cold.

II

Out of the silent portal of the hours,
When frosts are come and all the hosts put on

Their burnished gear to march across the night
And o'er a darkened earth in splendor shine,
Slowly above the world Orion wheels
His glittering square, while on the shadowy hill
And throbbing like a sea-light through the dusk,
Great Sirius rises in his flashing blue.
Lord of the winter night, august and pure,
Returning year on year untouched by time.
To kindle faith with thy immortal fire,
There are no hurts that beauty cannot ease,
No ills that love cannot at last repair,
In the courageous progress of the soul.

III

Russet and white and gray is the oak wood
In the great snow. Still from the North it comes,
Whispering, settling, sifting through the trees,
O'erloading branch and twig. The road is lost.
Clearing and meadow, stream and ice-bound pond
Are made once more a trackless wilderness
In the white hush where not a creature stirs;
And the pale sun is blotted from the sky.
In that strange twilight the lone traveller halts
To listen while the stealthy snowflakes fall.
And then far off toward the Stamford shore,
Where through the storm the coastwise liners go,
Faint and recurrent on the muffled air,
A foghorn booming through the smother, — hark!

IV

When the day changed and the mad wind died down,
The powdery drifts that all day long had blown

Across the meadows and the open fields,
Or whirled like diamond dust in the bright sun,
Settled to rest, and for a tranquil hour
The lengthening bluish shadows on the snow
Stole down the orchard slope, and a rose light
Flooded the earth with glory and with peace.
Then in the west behind the cedars black
The sinking sun made red the winter dusk
With sudden flare along the snowy ridge, —
Like a rare masterpiece by Hokusai,
Where on a background gray, with flaming breath
The crimson dragon dies in dusky gold.
The Nation   *Bliss Carman*

101   *The Twelve-Forty-Five*

(*For Edward J. Wheeler*)

WITHIN the Jersey City shed
The engine coughs and shakes its head.
The smoke, a plume of red and white,
Waves madly in the face of night.
And now the grave, incurious stars
Gleam on the groaning, hurrying cars.
Against the kind and awful reign
Of darkness, this our angry train,
A noisy little rebel, pouts
Its brief defiance, flames and shouts —
And passes on, and leaves no trace.
For darkness holds its ancient place,
Serene and absolute, the king
Unchanged, of every living thing.

OF MAGAZINE VERSE

The houses lie obscure and still
In Rutherford and Carlton Hill.
Our lamps intensify the dark
Of slumbering Passaic Park.
And quiet holds the weary feet
That daily tramp through Prospect Street.
What though we clang and clank and roar
Through all Passaic's streets?   No door
Will open, not an eye will see
Who this loud vagabond may be.
Upon my crimson cushioned seat,
In manufactured light and heat,
I feel unnatural and mean.
Outside the towns are cool and clean;
Curtained awhile from sound and sight
They take God's gracious gift of night.
The stars are watchful over them.
On Clifton as on Bethlehem
The angels, leaning down the sky,
Shed peace and gentle dreams.   And I —
I ride, I blasphemously ride
Through all the silent countryside.
The engine's shriek, the headlight's glare,
Pollute the still nocturnal air.
The cottages of Lake View sigh
And sleeping, frown as we pass by.
Why, even strident Paterson
Rests quietly as any nun.
Her foolish warring children keep
The grateful armistice of sleep.
For what tremendous errand's sake
Are we so blatantly awake?

What precious secret is our freight?
What king must be abroad so late?
Perhaps Death roams the hills to-night
And we rush forth to give him fight.
Or else, perhaps, we speed his way
To some remote unthinking prey.
Perhaps a woman writhes in pain
And listens — listens for the train!
The train, that like an angel sings,
The train, with healing on its wings.
Now "Hawthorne!" the conductor cries.
My neighbor starts and rubs his eyes.
He hurries yawning through the car
And steps out where the houses are.
This is the reason of our quest!
Not wantonly we break the rest
Of town and village, nor do we
Lightly profane night's sanctity.
What Love commands the train fulfils,
And beautiful upon the hills
Are these our feet of burnished steel.
Subtly and certainly I feel
That Glen Rock welcomes us to her
And silent Ridgewood seems to stir
And smile, because she knows the train
Has brought her children back again.
We carry people home — and so
God speeds us, wheresoe'er we go.
Hohokus, Waldwick, Allendale
Lift sleepy heads to give us hail.
In Ramsey, Mahwah, Suffern, stand
Houses that wistfully demand

A father — son — some human thing
That this, the midnight train, may bring.
The trains that travel in the day
They hurry folks to work or play.
The midnight train is slow and old
But of it let this thing be told,
To its high honor be it said,
It carries people home to bed.
My cottage lamp shines white and clear.
God bless the train that brought me here!
The Smart Set   *Joyce Kilmer*

102   *Coming Home*

THEY have hauled in the gang-plank. The breast-
   line crawls back.
It is "Port, and hard over!" and out through the black
Of the storm and the night, and across to the mouth
Of the harbor, where stretching far out to the south,
Run the lights of the town.

                          Swinging slowly we turn,
Pointing out for mid-lake, past the long pier where burn
The red harbor-lights, where the great billows churn
Blow on blow on the spiles, spilling down the white foam —
But I've written the home-folks that I'm coming home.

And I'm coming; huddled close by the slow-falling rail,
Blinking red through the mist and the spray, while the
   hail

Rattles down the wet decks lifting high, with the wail
Up the wind of the fog-horn and behind on our trail,
And we nose straight out in the teeth of the gale,
I know by the throb that the engines prevail,
And — steady, my courage — unless the stars fail,
We'll make it.

                But tell me, O gray eyes and blue,
Did you know in your watching, O dim eyes and true,
In that black night's wild fury while the storm-signals flew,
While the storm beat us back and the hoarse whistles blew —
Did you know, O my dear ones, I was coming to you?

The silence of midnight; the hiss of the swell;
The creaking of timbers; the close cabin smell;
The slow-swaying shadows; the jar of the screw;
The wind at the shutter; the feet of the crew;
The cry of a child — is he coming home, too?

There's a rent in the night and a star glimmers through.
The skies clear above us; the west banks up brown;
The wind dies across us; the sea's running down;
And across the dim water, still breaking in foam,
Stretches out the far shore-line — and I'm coming home.

The hills smile a welcome; the long night is past;
And the ship's turning into the harbor at last.
The engines slow down; we steal through the slip,
Past the low burning lamp and with quivering lip
Call down to the life-savers cheering us on.

OF MAGAZINE VERSE

The weary throb sends us straight into the dawn,
Fair and white up the bay, half asleep, all adream,
In its translucent purple and pearl. Just a gleam
Out there of the earliest sail; here the curl
Of the first lazy smoke from a cabin — a girl
Loops up the long vines at the doorway. A swirl
Of white water behind us; then a stir at the dock.
Steam slowly! The headline — the stern-line — the shock
As we swing alongside, and across the plank flock
Wan faces, with breath still a-quiver, the roar
Of the night still above and about them, the floor
Still uncertain; but over the grateful brown loam
We crowd to the shore-boat — and I'm coming home.

And away to the north over depths of cool green
From the bluffs overhead, where the deep-set ravine
Digs down to the heart of the wood, while a stream
Trickles out over sands drifting white, and the pier
Reaches out through the water to meet us. We're here!

From the pier to the boat-house and away down the shore
Flutters back to the group at the old farm-house door
The word that I'm coming. And from wrinkled old
    hands,
As the dear old feet toil through the weary white sands,
Bringing welcome and welcome, from boat-house and
    strand,
The hurrying, white-winged signals all come —
God pity the mortal who has never come home!

And I? I'm not worth it. But gray eyes and blue,
While the storms beat about me, O dear hearts and true,

Or the fogs flinging far, blot the stars from the blue,
If the pole star leads on or the rudder swings true,
It's not Heaven I'm after, I am coming to you.

But Heaven it will be when down the blue dome
Flutter out the white signals that I'm coming home.
    The Century Magazine   Elizabeth Sewell Hill

103   We who were Lovers of Life

From " The Story of Eleusis "

WE who were lovers of life, who were fond of the hearth and the homeland,
Gone like a drowner's cry borne on the perilous wind,
Gone from the glow of the sunlight, now are in exile eternal,
Strangers sit in the place dear to us once as our own.

Happy are they; and they know not we were as strangers before them;
Nay, nor that others shall come: Knowledge belongs to the dead.
Life is so rich that the living look not away from the present;
Eyes that the sun made blind learn in the dusk to see.

Once we had friends, we had kindred; all of us now are forgotten,
All but the hero-kings, lords of the glory of war;

These, with the founders of cities, live for a little in stories
Told of the deeds they did, not of the men that they
    were.

Those who were mighty but linger, shadowy forms in a
    legend;
Never the minstrel's tale tells what they were to their
    wives.
None on the lips of remembrance live as their children
    knew the1
Merged in the darkness kings rank with the recordless
    dead.

Whether our lifetime brought to us joy or the burden of
    sorrow,
Whether in youth or age, all when we come from the
    earth
Clinging to memories wander slow through the shadow-
    less meadows,
Dash from the proffered cup Lethe's oblivious draught.

Long are the years and uncounted passed in the season-
    less twilight
Thinking of things that were, feeling the ache of regret;
Slowly the echoes fade and the homeland hills are for-
    gotten:
Over the flame-swept waste waters of healing are poured.

Lovers of action, lovers of sunlight, rovers of ocean,
Shepherds, tillers of earth, yea, at the last we forget.
Longer a woman remembers words that were uttered in
    moonlight,
Girlhood's vision and dream, pitiful things of the home.

Here by the rivers of Hades; Phlegethon, Acheron, Lethe,
Wisdom comes, and the dead judge what they did with
    their lives:
Never the clustering vineyard yielded to any its fulness —
Ah, but the children here playing their desolate games!
    The Poetry Review of America   Louis V. Ledoux

104   *Summons*

THE eager night and the impetuous winds,
    The hints and whispers of a thousand lures,
And all the swift persuasion of the Spring,
Surged from the stars and stones, and swept me on. . . .
The smell of honeysuckles, keen and clear,
Startled and shook me, with the sudden thrill
Of some well-known but half-forgotten voice.
A slender stream became a naked sprite,
Flashed around curious bends, and winked at me
Beyond the turns, alert and mischievous.
A saffron moon, dangling among the trees,
Seemed like a toy balloon caught in the boughs,
Flung there in sport by some too-mirthful breeze. . . .
And as it hung there, vivid and unreal,
The whole world's lethargy was brushed away;
The night kept tugging at my torpid mood
And tore it into shreds. A warm air blew
My wintry slothfulness beyond the stars;
And over all indifference there streamed
A myriad urges in one rushing wave. . . .
Touched with the lavish miracles of earth,
I felt the brave persistence of the grass;

The far desire of rivulets; the keen,
Unconquerable fervor of the thrush;
The endless labors of the patient worm;
The lichen's strength; the prowess of the ant;
The constancy of flowers; the blind belief
Of ivy climbing slowly toward the sun;
The eternal struggles and eternal deaths —
And yet the groping faith of every root!
Out of old graves arose the cry of life;
Out of the dying came the deathless call.
And, thrilling with a new sweet restlessness,
The thing that was my boyhood woke in me —
Dear, foolish fragments made me strong again;
Valiant adventures, dreams of those to come,
And all the vague, heroic hopes of youth,
With fresh abandon, like a fearless laugh,
Leaped up to face the heaven's unconcern. . . .

And then — veil upon veil was torn aside —
Stars, like a host of merry girls and boys,
Danced gaily 'round me, plucking at my hand;
The night, scorning its ancient mystery,
Leaned down and pressed new courage in my heart;
The hermit-thrush, throbbing with more Song,
Sang with a happy challenge to the skies;
Love, and the faces of a world of children,
Swept like a conquering army through my blood —
And Beauty, rising out of all its forms,
Beauty, the passion of the universe,
Flamed with its joy, a thing too great for tears,
And, like a wine, poured itself out for me
To drink of, to be warmed with, and to go

Refreshed and strengthened to the ceaseless fight;
To meet with confidence the cynic years;
Battling in wars that never can be won,
Seeking the lost cause and the brave defeat.
The Century Magazine　　　　　*Louis Untermeyer*

105　　　　　The Dead

I

THINK you the dead are lonely in that place?
　　They are companioned by the leaves and grass,
By many a beautiful and vanished face,
　　By all the strange and lovely things that pass.
Sunsets and dawnings and the starry vast,
　　The swimming moon, the tracery of trees —
These they shall know more perfectly at last,
　　They shall be intimate with such as these.
'T is only for the living Beauty dies,
　　Fades and drifts from us with too brief a grace,
Beyond the changing tapestry of skies
　　Where dwells her perfect and immortal face.
For us the passage brief: — the happy dead
　　Are ever by great beauty visited.

II

All Souls' Night!　Forth from their dwelling places
　　They cross the aching and uneasy night,
Seeking old doors and dear remembered faces,
　　Peering unseen in windows where a light

Falls on some book they loved or on some chair
  Where they had rested many a night ago;
And well for them if one dear face be there
  Whose unforgetting eyes they knew — and know.
Ah, well for them if in the quiet speech
  That passes round the low-burned candle flame,
Some old familiar tale the listeners reach,
  And silence fall about a spoken name. —
Better their sleep in those dim dwelling places,
  For finding remembered and remembering faces.
The Forum   David Morton

106   *We Dead*

WHEN from the brooding home,
  The silent immemorial love-house,
The belovèd body of the mother in her travail,
Naked, the little one comes and wails at the world's bleak weather,
We say that on Earth and to us a child has been born. . . .
But now we move with unhalting pace toward the dark evening,
And toward the cold lengthening shadow,
And quick we avert our fearful eyes from the strange event,
The burial and the bourne . . .
That leaving home: the end . . . death. . . .

Are these then birth and death?
Does the cut of a cord bring life and dust to dust expunge it?
If so, what are we then, we dead?

For, in the cities,
And dark on the lonely farms, and waifs on the ocean,
As a harrying of wind, as an eddying of dust,
We dead, in our soft shining bodies that are combed and
    are kissed,
Are ghosts fleeing from the inescapable hell of ourselves . . .

We are even as beetles skating over the waters of our
    own darkness,
Even as beetles, darting and restless,
But the depths dark and void . . .

We have found no peace, no peace: though our engines
    are crafty:
What avail wings to the flier in the skies
While his dead soul like an anchor drags on the Earth?
And what avails lightning darting a man's voice, linking
    the cities,
While in the booth he is the same varnished clod,
And his soul flies not after?
And what avails it that the body of man has waxed
    mammoth,
Limbed with the lightning and the stream,
While his spirit remains a torment and a trifle,
And gaining the world, profits nothing?

Self-murdered, self-slain, the dead cumber the Earth. . . .
And how did they die?

A boy was born in the pouring radiance of creative magic:
And with pulses of music he was born . . .
Of himself he might have been shaping a song-wingèd
    poet . . .
But he was afraid. . . .

He feared the gaunt garret of starvation and the lonely
      years in his soul's desert,
And he feared to be a jest and a fool before his friends. . . .
Now he clerks, the slave . . .
And the magic is slimed with disastrous opiates of the Night.

A girl was bathed with the lissome beauty of the seeker
      of love,
The call of the animals one to another in the Spring,
The desire of the captive woman in her heart, as she ran
      and leaped on the hills;
But the imprisoned beast's cry terrified her as she looked
      out over the love-quiet of the modern world . . .
Yet she desired to take this man-lure and release it into
      loveliness,
Become a dancer, lulling with witchcraft of her young
      body the fevered world
But, no, her mother spied here a wickedness. . . .
Shamefully she submitted, making a smoldering inferno
      of the hidden Nymph in her soul,
And so died.

A woman was made body and heart for the beautiful
      love-life. . . .
But of the mother-miracle,
How the cry of a troubled child whitens the red passions,
She did not know. . . .
Fear of poverty corrupted her: she chose a fool that her
      heart hated,
And now through him no release for her native passions,
But only a spending of her loathsome fury on adornment
      and luxury. . . .
Ah, dead glory! and the heart sick with betrayal!

There is no grace for the dead, save to be born again:
Engines shall not drag us from the grave,
Nor wine nor meat revive us.

For our thirst is a thirst no liquor can reach nor slake,
And our hunger a hunger by no bread filled. . . .
The waters we crave bubble up from the springs of life,
And the bread we would break comes down from invisible hands.

We dead! awake!
Kiss the belovèd past goodby,
Go leave the love-house of the betrayèd self,
And through the dark of birth go and enter the soul's bleak weather. . . .
And I, I will not stay dead, though the dead cling to me,
I will put away the kisses and the soft embraces and the walls that encompass me,
And out of this womb I will surely move to the world of my spirit. . . .
I will lose my life to find it, as of old,
Yea, I will turn from the life-lie I lived to the truth I was wrought for,
And I will take the creator within, sower of the seed of the race,
And make him a god, shaper of civilization. . . .

Now on my soul's imperious surge,
Taking the risk, as of death, and in deepening twilight,
I ride on the darkening flood and go out on the waters

Till over the tide comes music, till over the tide the
    breath
Of the song of my far-off soul is wafted and blown,
Murmuring commandments. . . .

Storm and darkness! I am drowned in the torrent!
I am moving forth irrevocably from the sheltering womb!
I am naked and little!
Oh, cold of the world, and light blinding, and space
    terrifying!
Now my cry goes up and the wailing of my helpless soul:
Mother, my mother!

Lo, then, the mother eternal!
In my opening soul the footfall of her fleeting tread,
And the song of her voice piercing and sweet with love of
    me,
And the enwinding of her arms and adoring of her breath,
And the milk of her plenty!
Oh, Life, of which I am part; Life, from the depths of
    the heavens,
That ascended like a water-spring into David of Asia on
    the eastern hills in the night,
That came like a noose of golden shadow on Joan in the
    orchard,
That gathers all life: the binding of brothers into sheaves,
That of old, kneelers in the dust
Named, glorying: Allah, Jehovah, God.
   The Century Magazine   *James Oppenheim*

107   *To a Dead Soldier*

THOUGH all the primrose paths of morning called
   Your feet to follow them, and all the winds
Of all the hills of earth, with plucking hands
Wooed you to slopes that shone like emerald,
   You might not go. The thin green grass that binds
Your feet had Earth and Death to forge its bands.

The rain's wet kiss is on your lips, where lay
   Once the live pulses of a woman's soul;
Your eyes give back unto the quiet sky
Only the sheen of stars, the glare of day,
   Or darkness when the kindly shadows roll
Up from the sea to hide you where you lie.

No woman's whisper holds your strong heart spent
   And breathless. All the silver horns that blew
While legions cheered, are still. These things are done,
But these you have: a death for monument,
   And peace you died to buy, and after you
The laughing play of children in the sun.
   The Eliot Literary Magazine   Kendall Harrison

108   *The Death of the Hired Man*

MARY sat musing on the lamp-flame at the table
   Waiting for Warren. When she heard his step,
She ran on tip-toe down the darkened passage
To meet him in the doorway with the news
And put him on his guard. "Silas is back."

She pushed him outward with her through the door
And shut it after her. "Be kind," she said.
She took the market things from Warren's arms
And set them on the porch, then drew him down
To sit beside her on the wooden steps.

"When was I ever anything but kind to him?
But I'll not have the fellow back," he said.
"I told him so last haying, did n't I?
'If he left then,' I said, 'that ended it.'
What good is he? Who else will harbor him
At his age for the little he can do?
What help he is there's no depending on.
Off he goes always when I need him most.
'He thinks he ought to earn a little pay,
Enough at least to buy tobacco with,
So he won't have to beg and be beholden.'
'All right,' I say, 'I can't afford to pay
Any fixed wages, though I wish I could.'
'Someone else can.' 'Then someone else will have to.'

"I should n't mind his bettering himself
If that was what it was. You can be certain,
When he begins like that, there's someone at him
Trying to coax him off with pocket-money, —
In haying time, when any help is scarce.
In winter he comes back to us. I'm done."

"Sh! not so loud: he'll hear you," Mary said.
"I want him to: he'll have to soon or late."

"He's worn out. He's asleep beside the stove.
When I came up from Rowe's I found him here,

Huddled against the barn-door fast asleep,
A miserable sight, and frightening, too —
You need n't smile — I did n't recognize him —
I was n't looking for him — and he's changed.
Wait till you see."

  "Where did you say he'd been?"

"He did n't say. I dragged him to the house,
And gave him tea and tried to make him smoke.
I tried to make him talk about his travels.
Nothing would do: he just kept nodding off."

"What did you say? Did he say anything?"

"But little."

  "Anything? Mary, confess
He said he'd come to ditch the meadow for me."

"Warren!"

  "But did he? I just want to know."

"Of course he did. What would you have him say?
Surely you would n't grudge the poor old man
Some humble way to save his self-respect.
He added, if you really care to know,
He meant to clear the upper pasture, too.
That sounds like something you have heard before?
Warren, I wish you could have heard the way
He jumbled everything. I stopped to look
Two or three times — he made me feel so queer —
To see if he was talking in his sleep.

He ran on Harold Wilson — you remember —
The boy you had in haying four years since.
He's finished school, and teaching in his college.
Silas declares you'll have to get him back.
He says they two will make a team for work:
Between them they will lay this farm as smooth!
The way he mixed that in with other things.
He thinks young Wilson a likely lad, though daft
On education — you know how they fought
All through July under the blazing sun,
Silas up on the cart to build the load,
Harold along beside to pitch it on."

"Yes, I took care to keep well out of earshot."

"Well, those days trouble Silas like a dream.
You would n't think they would. How some things linger!
Harold's young college boy's assurance piqued him.
After so many years he still keeps finding
Good arguments he sees he might have used.
I sympathize. I know just how it feels
To think of the right thing to say too late.
Harold's associated in his mind with Latin.
He asked me what I thought of Harold's saying
He studied Latin like the violin
Because he liked it — that an argument!
He said he could n't make the boy believe
He could find water with a hazel prong —
Which showed how much good school had ever done him.
He wanted to go over that. But most of all
He th: if he could have another chance
To teach him how to build a load of hay —"

"I know, that's Silas' one accomplishment.
He bundles every forkful in its place,
And tags and numbers it for future reference,
So he can find and easily dislodge it
In the unloading. Silas does that well.
He takes it out in bunches like big birds' nests.
You never see him standing on the hay
He's trying to lift, straining to lift himself."

"He thinks if he could teach him that, he'd be
Some good perhaps to someone in the world.
He hates to see a boy the fool of books.
Poor Silas, so concerned for other folks,
And nothing to look backward to with pride,
And nothing to look forward to with hope,
So now and never any different."

Part of a moon was falling down the west,
Dragging the whole sky with it to the hills.
Its light poured softly in her lap. She saw
And spread her apron to it. She put out her hand
Among the harp-like morning-glory strings,
Taut with the dew from garden bed to eaves,
As if she played unheard the tenderness
That wrought on him beside her in the night.
"Warren," she said, "he has come home to die:
You need n't be afraid he'll leave you this time."

"Home," he mocked gently.

      "Yes, what else but home?
It all depends on what you mean by home.
Of course he's nothing to us, any more
Than was the hound that came a stranger to us
Out of the woods, worn out upon the trail."

"Home is the place where, when you have to go there,
They have to take you in."

                                          "I should have called it
Something you somehow have n't to deserve."

Warren leaned out and took a step or two,
Picked up a little stick, and brought it back.
And broke it in his hand and tossed it by.
"Silas has better claim on us you think
Than on his brother? Thirteen little miles
As the road winds would bring him to his door.
Silas has walked that far no doubt to-day.
Why did n't he go there? His brother's rich,
A somebody — director in the bank."

"He never told us that."

                                         "We know it though."

"I think his brother ought to help, of course.
I'll see to that if there is need. He ought of right
To take him in, and might be willing to —
He may be better than appearances.
But have some pity on Silas. Do you think
If he'd had any pride in claiming kin
Or anything he looked for from his brother,
He'd keep so still about him all this time?"

"I wonder what's between them?"

                                         "I can tell you.
Silas is what he is — we would n't mind him —
But just the kind that kinsfolk can't abide.

He never did a thing so very bad.
He don't know why he is n't quite as good
As anyone. He won't be made ashamed
To please his brother, worthless though he is."

"*I* can't think Si ever hurt anyone."

"No, but he hurt my heart the way he lay
And rolled his old head on that sharp-edged chair-back.
He would n't let me put him on the lounge.
You must go in and see what you can do.
I made the bed up for him there to-night.
You 'll be surprised at him — how much he's broken.
His working days are done; I 'm sure of it."

"I 'd not be in a hurry to say that."

"I have n't been. Go, look, see for yourself.
But, Warren, please remember how it is:
He 's come to help you ditch the meadow.
He has a plan. You must n't laugh at him.
He may not speak of it, and then he may.
I 'll sit and see if that small sailing cloud
Will hit or miss the moon."

                          It hit the moon.
Then there were three there, making a dim row,
The moon, the little silver cloud, and she.

Warren returned — too soon, it seemed to her,
Slipped to her side, caught up her hand and waited.

"Warren," she questioned.

                  "Dead," was all he answered.

The New Republic   *Robert Frost*

109 *A Handful of Dust*

I STOOPED to the silent Earth and lifted a handful of
  her dust. . . .
Was it a handful of humanity I held?
Was it the crumbled and blown beauty of a woman or a
  babe?
For over the hills of Earth blows the dust of the withered
  generations;
And not a water-drop in the sea but was once a blood-
  drop or a tear:
And not an atom of sap in leaf or bud but was once the
  love-sap in a human being:
And not a lump of soil but was once the rosy curve of lip
  or breast or cheek. . . .

Handful of dust, you stagger me . . .
I did not dream the world was so full of the dead:
And the air I breathe so rich with the bewildering past:
Kiss of what girls is on the wind?
Whisper of what lips is in the cup of my hand?
Cry of what deaths is in the break of the wave tossed by
  the sea?
I am enfolded in an air of rushing wings:
I am engulfed in clouds of love-lives gone. . . .
Who leans yonder? Helen of Greece?
Who walks with me? Isolde?
The trees are shaking down the blossoms from Juliet's
  breast:
And the bee drinks honey from the lips of David. . .

Come, girl, my comrade:
Stand close, sun-tanned one, with your bright eyes lifted:
Behold this dust . . .
This is you: this of the Earth under our feet is you:
Raised by what miracle? shaped by what magic?
Breathed into by what god?
And a hundred years hence one like myself may come,
And stoop, and take a handful of the yielding Earth,
And never dream that in his palm
Lies she that laughed and ran and lived beside this sea
On an afternoon a hundred years before. . . .

Listen to the dust in this hand:
Who is trying to speak to us?
   The Century Magazine   *James Oppenheim*

110 *"I Have a Rendezvous with Death"*

I HAVE a rendezvous with Death
  At some disputed barricade,
When Spring comes back with rustling shade
And apple-blossoms fill the air —
I have a rendezvous with Death
When Spring brings back blue days and fair.

It may be he shall take my hand
And lead me into his dark land
And close my eyes and quench my breath —
It may be I shall pass him still.
I have a rendezvous with Death
On some scarred slope of battered hill,

When Spring comes round again this year
And the first meadow-flowers appear.

God knows 't were better to be deep
Pillowed in silk and scented down,
Where love throbs out in blissful sleep,
Pulse nigh to pulse, and breath to breath,
Where hushed awakenings are dear . . .
But I've a rendezvous with Death
At midnight in some flaming town,
When Spring trips north again this year,
And I to my pledged word am true,
I shall not fail that rendezvous.
The North American Review   *Alan Seeger*

111   *The Secret*

THEY drew the blinds down, and the house was old
With shadows, and so cold,
Filled up with shuddery silence like held breath.
And when I grew quite bold
And asked them why, they said that this was death.

They walked tiptoe about the house that day
And turned their heads away
Each time I passed. I sat down in surprise
And quite forgot to play,
Seeing them pass with wonder in their eyes.

My mother came into my room that night
Holding a shaded light

Above my face till she was sure I slept;
But I lay still with fright,
Hearing her breath, and knowing that she wept.

And afterward, with not a one to see,
I got up quietly
And tried each step I made with my bare feet
Until it seemed to me
That all the air grew sorrowful and sweet.

So without breathing I went down the stair,
In the light chilly air,
Into the parlor, where the perfumes led,
I lit my candle there
And held it a long time above my head.

There was an oblong box, and at its base
Grew lilies in a vase
As white as they. I thought them very tall
In such a listening place,
And they threw fearful shadows on the wall.

I tiptoed to the box, then, silently,
To look what death could be;
And then I smiled, for it was father who
Was sleeping quietly,
He dreamed, I think, for he was smiling, too.

And all at once I knew death is a thing
That stoops down, whispering
A dear, forgotten secret in your ear
Such as the winds can sing.
And then you sleep and dream and have no fear.

Perhaps the winds have told the dream to flowers
On nights of lonely hours;
Perhaps we, too, could learn if we could seek
The wind in his watch-towers;
Perhaps the lilies knew, but could not speak.
    The Century Magazine   *Frederick Faust*

112 *Scintilla*

I KISSED a kiss in youth
  Upon a dead man's brow;
And that was long ago, —
  And I'm a grown man now.

It's lain there in the dust,
  Thirty years and more: —
My lips that set a light
  At a dead man's door!

The Crisis   *William Stanley Braithwaite*

113 *Sleep*

I

WHERE do I go
  Down roads of sleep,
Behind the blue-brimmed day?
No more I know her silvered sweep
Nor colors clear nor gray,
Nor women's ways
Nor those of men,
Nor blame, nor praise.
Where am I, then?

II

Oh, fragrantly
The airs of earth arise
In waking hours of light,
While vagrantly
Sea symphonies
Of changing sound surprise;
Till for a space one goes
Beyond the salt and snows
And claimant tides along the wide-stretched beach,
Beyond the last, faint reach
Of odor, sight and sound, far forth — far forth —
Where neither South nor North
Points down the roads unguessed,
Where East is not, nor West:
At night down roads of sleep,
Of dreamless sleep,
Past all the compassed ways the reason tells,
To unknown citadels.

III

Just as one turns, and while day's dusk-breathed blue
And music, many-dappled, merge in flight,
Half in a dream, one finds a tale is true
That down one's memory sings, still and light.
Just as the spirit turns,
Half-dreaming one discerns
Deeply the tale is true
That long ago one knew:
Of how a mermaid loved a mortal knight;
And how, unless she died, she still must change,

And leave his human ways, and go alone
At intervals where seas unfathomed range
Through coral groves around the ocean's throne,
Where cool-armed mermaids dive through crystal hours,
And braid their streaming hair with pearls, and sing
Among the green and clear-lit water flowers,
The lucent splendors of their ocean king.

IV

Like hers our ways on earth,
Who, from our day of birth,
Would die, unless we slept —
Must die, unless for hours,
Beyond our senses' powers,
Down soundless space we leapt.

V

Beyond the deepest roll
Of pain's and rapture's sweep,
Where goes the human soul
That vanishes in sleep?

VI

Down dreamless paths unguessed, beyond the senses'
    powers,
Beyond the breath of fragrance, sound and light,
As once through crystal, unremembered hours
The mermaid dived who loved a mortal knight:
Far forth — far forth —
Beyond the South or North,

Past all the compassed ways the day has shown,
To live divine and deep at night down roads of sleep,
In citadels unknown.
    Poetry: A Magazine of Verse   *Edith Wyatt*

114   *A Memorial Tablet*

Oh, Agathocles, fare thee well!

NAKED and brave thou goest
    Without one glance behind!
Hast thou no fear, Agathocles,
    Or backward grief of mind?

The dreamy dog beside thee
    Presses against thy knee;
He, too, oh, sweet Agathocles,
    Is deaf and visioned like thee.

Thou art so lithe and lovely
    And yet thou art not ours.
What Delphic saying compels thee
    Of kings or topless towers?

That little blowing mantle
    Thou losest from thine arm —
No shoon nor staff, Agathocles,
    Nor sword, to fend from harm!

Thou hast the changed impersonal
    Awed brow of mystery —

Yesterday thou wast burning,
  Mad boy, for Glaucöe.

Philis thy mother calls thee:
  Mine eyes with tears are dim,
Turn once, look once, Agathocles —
  (*The gods have blinded him.*)

Come back, Agathocles, the night —
  Brings thee what place of rest?
Wine-sweet are Glaucöe's kisses,
  Flower-soft her budding breast.

He seems to hearken, Glaucöe,
  He seems to listen and smile;
(*Nay, Philis, but a god-song
He follows this many a mile.*)

Come back, come back, Agathocles!
  (*He scents the asphodel;
Unearthly swift he runneth.*)
  Agathocles, farewell!

Scribner's Magazine   *Florence Wilkinson Evans.*

115   *Epitaph*

HERE lies the flesh that tried
  To follow the spirit's leading;
Fallen at last, it died,
  Broken, bruised and bleeding,
Burned by the high fires
Of the spirit's desires.

It had no dream to sing
  Of ultimate liberty;
Fashioned for suffering,
  To endure transiently,
And conscious that it must
Return as dust to dust.

It blossomed a brief hour,
  Was rosy, warm and strong;
It went like a wilted flower,
  It ended like a song,
Some one closed a door —
And it was seen no more.

The grass is very kind;
  (It knows so many dead!)
Those whom it covers find
  Their wild hearts comforted;
Their pulses need not meet
The spirit's speed and heat.

Here lies the flesh that held
  The spirit prisoner —
A caged thing that rebelled,
  Forced to subminister;
Broken it had to be;
To set its captive free.

It is very glad to rest,
  It calls to roots and rain,

Safe in its mother's breast,
   Ready to bloom again.
   After a day and an hour
  'T will greet the sun a flower.

The New York Times   *Louise Driscoll*

116   *Comrades*

WHERE are the friends that I knew in my Maying,
   In the days of my youth, in the first of my roaming?
We were dear; we were leal; O, far we went straying;
   Now never a heart to my heart comes homing! —
Where is he now, the dark boy slender
   Who taught me bare-back, stirrup and reins?
I loved him; he loved me; my beautiful, tender
   Tamer of horses on grass-grown plains.

Where is he now whose eyes swam brighter,
   Softer than love, in his turbulent charms;
Who taught me to strike, and to fall, dear fighter,
   And gathered me up in his boyhood arms;
Taught me the rifle, and with me went riding,
   Suppled my limbs to the horseman's war;
Where is he now, for whom my heart's biding,
   Biding, biding — but he rides far!

O love that passes the love of woman!
   Who that hath felt it shall ever forget,
When the breath of life with a throb turns human,
   And a lad's heart is to a lad's heart set?

Ever, forever, lover and rover —
   They shall cling, nor each from other shall part
Till the reign of the stars in the heavens be over,
   And life is dust in each faithful heart!

They are dead, the American grasses under;
   There is no one now who presses my side;
By the African chotts I am riding asunder,
   And with great joy ride I the last great ride.
I am fey; I am fain of sudden dying;
   Thousands of miles there is no one near;
And my heart — all the night it is crying, crying
   In the bosoms of dead lads darling-dear.

Hearts of my music — them dark earth covers;
   Comrades to die, and to die for, were they;
In the width of the world there were no such rovers —
   Back to back, breast to breast, it was ours to stay;
And the highest on earth was the vow that we cherished,
   To spur forth from the crowd and come back never more,
And to ride in the track of great souls perished
   Till the nests of the lark shall roof us o'er.

Yet lingers a horseman on Altai highlands,
   Who hath joy of me, riding the Tartar glissade;
And one, far faring o'er orient islands
   Whose blood yet glints with my blade's accolade;
North, west, east, I fling you my last hallooing,
   Last love to the breasts where my own has bled;
Through the reach of the desert my soul leaps pursuing
   My star where it rises a Star of the Dead.

Scribner's Magazine   *George Edward Woodberry*

117 They went Forth to Battle, but they always Fell

THEY went forth to battle, but they always fell;
  Their eyes were fixed above the sullen shields;
Nobly they fought and bravely, but not well,
And sank heart-wounded by a subtle spell.
  They knew not fear that to the foeman yields,
  They were not weak, as one who vainly wields
A futile weapon; yet the sad scrolls tell
How on the hard-fought field they always fell.

It was a secret music that they heard,
  A sad sweet plea for pity and for peace;
And that which pierced the heart was but a word,
Though the white breast was red-lipped where the sword
  Pressed a fierce cruel kiss, to put surcease
  On its hot thirst, but drank a hot increase.
Ah, they by some strange troubling doubt were stirred,
And died for hearing what no foeman heard.

They went forth to battle but they alway fell;
  Their might was not the might of lifted spears;
Over the battle-clamor came a spell
Of troubling music, and they fought not well.
  Their wreaths are willows and their tribute, tears;
  Their names are old sad stories in men's ears;
Yet they will scatter the red Hordes of Hell,
Who went forth to battle and always fell.

The Forum   *Shaemas O Sheel*

118   *The Unknown Brothers*

SINGING band by song united
    When the blue Ægean plains
Girdled isles where lovers lighted
    Lamps in Kypris' seaward fanes;
Singing Brothers, earth enfolden,
What of you and of your olden
    Music now? What still remains?

Scattered blooms, surviving only
    As the petal holds the rose,
In the garden where the lonely
    Scarlet flower of Sappho blows;
And of some no single token —
Leaf or bud, or blossom broken —
    Now the mounded garden shows.

Was there lack of exaltation
    In the burden of their song?
Had they less of consecration?
    Proved the path of Beauty long?
Did they pause for pleasant resting?
Swerve or falter in their questing?
    Have the ages done them wrong?

Some there may have been who faltered
    By the bright Ægean foam,
Seeing life with vision altered
    As the soul forgot its home;

OF MAGAZINE VERSE

Some it may be in confusion,
After youth's divine illusion,
   Turned to till the kindly loam.

Some there are in all the ages
   Lonely vigil fail to keep;
Some allured by wisdom's pages
   Chart the sky and sound the deep;
Some give up the long foregoing —
Human touches, reaping, sowing —
   Some with Sappho take the leap.

But the most wait unrepining,
   Hopeful when all hope is fled,
For fulfilment of the shining
   Dawn that lingers far ahead,
And, by paths of no returning
Where the hearth-fires are not burning,
   March companioned by the dead.

Through neglect or loud derision,
   Mocked at by the worldly-wise,
Bearing burdens of misprision,
   Seeking truth and finding lies,
Follow they the glow or glimmer
Of the vision growing dimmer
   As the death-mist fills their eyes.

Never can you be requited,
   Unknown Brothers, staunch and brave;
You the bitter gods have slighted,
   Only half their gift they gave,

Gave the patience of endeavor,
Kept fruition back forever,
　Felled the cypress by your grave.

You are passed, but unknown brothers,
　Finding faith of small avail,
Follow now as followed others,
　And I pause to bid them hail.
Brothers are they in believing,
Some it may be are achieving,
　But they triumph though they fail.

The Bookman   *Louis V. Ledoux*

119   The Monk in the Kitchen

I

ORDER is a lovely thing;
　On disarray it lays its wing,
Teaching simplicity to sing.
It has a meek and lowly grace,
Quiet as a nun's face.
Lo — I will have thee in this place!
Tranquil well of deep delight,
Transparent as the water, bright —
All things that shine through thee appear
As stones through water, sweetly clear
Thou clarity,
That with angelic charity
Revealest beauty where thou art,
Spread thyself like a clean pool.

Then all the things that in thee are,
Shall seem more spiritual and fair,
Reflection from serener air —
Sunken shapes of many a star
In the high heavens set afar.

II

Ye stolid, homely, visible things,
Above you all brood glorious wings
Of your deep entities, set high,
Like slow moons in a hidden sky.
But you, their likenesses, are spent
Upon another element.
Truly ye are but seemings —
The shadowy cast-off gleamings
Of bright solidities. Ye seem
Soft as water, vague as dream;
Image, cast in a shifting stream.

III

What are ye?
I know not.
Brazen pan and iron pot,
Yellow brick and gray flag-stone
That my feet have trod upon —
Ye seem to me
Vessels of bright mystery.
For ye do bear a shape, and so
Though ye were made by man, I know
An inner Spirit also made
And ye his breathings have obeyed.

IV

Shape, the strong and awful Spirit,
Laid his ancient hand on you.
He waste chaos doth inherit;
He can alter and subdue.
Verily, he doth lift up
Matter, like a sacred cup.
Into deep substance he reached, and lo
Where ye were not, ye were; and so
Out of useless nothing, ye
Groaned and laughed and came to be.
And I use you, as I can,
Wonderful uses, made for man,
Iron pot and brazen pan.

V

What are ye?
I know not;
Nor what I really do
When I move and govern you.
There is no small work unto God.
He requires of us greatness;
Of his least creature
A high angelic nature,
Stature superb and bright completeness.
He sets to us no humble duty.
Each act that he would have us do
Is haloed round with strangest beauty
Terrific deeds and cosmic tasks
Of his plainest child he asks.
When I polish the brazen pan

I hear a creature laugh afar
In the gardens of a star,
And from his burning presence run
Flaming wheels of many a sun.
Whoever makes a thing more bright,
He is an angel of all light.
When I cleanse this earthen floor
My spirit leaps to see
Bright garments trailing over it,
A cleanness made by me.
Purger of all men's thoughts and ways,
With labor do I sound Thy praise,
My work is done for Thee.
Whoever makes a thing more bright,
He is an angel of all light.
Therefore let me spread abroad
The beautiful cleanness of my God.

VI

One time in the cool of dawn
Angels came and worked with me.
The air was soft with many a wing.
They laughed amid my solitude
And cast bright looks on everything.
Sweetly of me did they ask
That they might do my common task
And all were beautiful — but one
With garments whiter than the sun
Had such a face
Of deep, remembered grace;
That when I saw. I cried — "Thou art
The great Blood-Brother of my heart.

Where have I seen thee?" — And he said,
"When we are dancing round God's throne,
How often thou art there.
Beauties from thy hands have flown
Like white doves wheeling in mid air.
Nay — thy soul remembers not?
Work on, and cleanse thy iron pot."

VII

What are we?   I know not.
The Craftsman   *Anna Hempstead Branch*

120   *Doors*

LIKE a young child who at his mother's door
    Runs eager for the welcoming embrace,
And finds the door shut, and with troubled face
Calls and through sobbing calls, and o'er and o'er
Calling, storms at the panel — so before
    A door that will not open, sick and numb,
    I listen for a word that will not come,
And know at last, I may not enter more.

Silence! And through the silence and the dark
    By that closed door, the distant sob of tears
    Beats on my spirit, as on fairy shores
The spectral sea; and through the sobbing, hark!
    Down the fair-chambered corridor of years,
    The quiet shutting, one by one, of doors.
The North American Review   *Hermann Hagedorn*

www.ingramcontent.com/pod-product-compliance
Lightning Source LLC
Chambersburg PA
CBHW021200230426
43667CB00006B/490